I0462017

Andreas Sofroniou

Andreas Sofroniou

HISTORY OF COMPUTER PROGRAMS

ISBN: 978-0-244-64246-4

Andreas Sofroniou, 2017 © Copyright

Andreas Sofroniou, 2017 © Copyright

HISTORY OF COMPUTER PROGRAMS

ISBN: 978-0-244-64246-4

CONTENTS   PAGE

Andreas Sofroniou

Andreas Sofroniou

Andreas Sofroniou

COMPUTER, HISTORY OF

Development of computers

Although the development of the computer has been largely played out during the 20th century, there is a long history of automatic calculation. Hero wrote in the 1st century AD of representing numbers using a train of gears, but little real progress seems to have been made until the early 17th century, when the first calculators were built, and the German mathematician Gottfried Leibniz speculated (1679) on the possibility of building a calculator using moving balls to represent numbers in binary code.

The notion of storing a sequence of instructions mechanically is also very old and was incorporated into self-playing musical

9

instruments and other automata even in ancient times. In 1725 Basile Bouchon invented a method of producing intricate woven patterns on a draw loom from instructions on a perforated paper tape. By 1800 this method had been refined by Jacquard into a highly successful automatic loom controlled by punched cards. The idea of punched-card instructions was adapted by Hollerith to record and analyse the results of the 1890 US census in the earliest example of large-scale data processing.

In 1835 Babbage conceived of the basic idea of an analytical engine in which can be found most of the elements of a truly general-purpose computer. He drew together the ideas of mechanical calculation and a set of instructions recorded on perforated paper tape.

The development costs of the machine were very high: the British government eventually

10

withdrew funding, and this pioneering machine was never completed. Babbage's ideas were subsequently lost until the 1930s, when work on electromechanical computers was started independently in Germany and the USA. In 1941 Konrad Zuse in Germany built the world's first working stored-program computer. His Z3 machine was based on electromechanical relays, and was used for military aircraft design. In the USA, the mathematician Howard Aiken, in association with IBM (International Business Machines), was working independently on a large electromechanical calculator that could be programmed using paper tape.

The Automatic Sequence Controlled Calculator (ASCC), or Harvard Mark I, was completed in 1943; it was very similar in concept (although not in engineering realization), to Babbage's analytical machine.

11

Computers based on the electronic thermionic valve were a major development, since they were much faster and more reliable than electromechanical computers. Among the earliest electronic computers were the Colossus series of special-purpose computers, developed secretly in the UK from 1943. They deciphered coded German messages produced on sophisticated mechanical systems called Enigma machines.

An important member of the Colossus team was Turing, who in 1936 had published a paper that defined in abstract terms the generalized concept of a universal computer. The concept of the stored-program computer (an idea attributed to von Neumann), in which instructions for processing data are stored along with the data in the computer's own memory, proved to be very important, since it hugely enhanced the flexibility and potential of the computer.

The earliest electronic stored-program computer was an experimental machine built under the leadership of Frederick Williams at Manchester University, UK, in 1948. This was followed by the Manchester Mark 1 computer in 1949 which, as the Ferranti Mark 1, was the first commercially available computer to be delivered. Other notable early computers in the UK were EDSAC at Cambridge, later marketed as LEO, and Turing's ACE at the National Physical Laboratory.

Mauchly and Eckert at the University of Pennsylvania (USA) developed the ENIAC and EDVAC computers based on the highly influential ideas of von Neumann; they later developed the successful UNIVAC computer, which became commercially available in 1951.

The development of the transistor led to much cheaper, faster, and more reliable computers. The first transistorized computer was working at Manchester University in 1953, although the USA had a number of much larger computers operating within a few years.

The first compiler was developed at Manchester in 1952, and in 1954 John Backus of IBM in the USA developed FORTRAN, the first internationally used computer language. A significant high point in this era was the joint development of the Atlas computer by Ferranti Ltd. and Manchester University. This was the world's first super-computer, and pioneered many aspects of computer architecture that are common today.

After this, most major developments took place in the USA. Particularly crucial was the development of the integrated circuit (IC) in 1958 which allowed complete circuits to be manufactured on a tiny piece of silicon. In 1972 the Intel Corporation developed the world's first microprocessor, the Intel 4004, which was very limited but was an immediate commercial success and led directly to the development of today's cheap, fast, and reliable microcomputer as well as much more powerful mainframe computers.

Computer

The term computer as normally used is for a device storing and processing data, according to a program of instructions stored within the computer itself. The term computer normally refers to electronic digital computers, but analogue computers also exist for use in specialist applications.

Computers are 'universal' information-processing machines: any information-processing task that can be specified by an algorithm (a well-defined sequence of instructions) can, in principle, be performed by a computer.

Unlike most other machines, it is not necessary to build a new computer for each

15

new task. Computers can therefore perform a very large number of useful tasks, although limits do exist: it can be proved that some problems are incomputable.

The mathematical study of what tasks are capable of being computed is known as compatibility, and complexity is the study of how hard it is to compute a task. Numerical analysis concerns the fastest and most accurate way to solve numerical problems.

The digital computer is one of the most significant innovations of the 20th century (see computer, history of). In the four decades since its introduction it has had an impact on almost all areas of human activity (see information technology).

Computers are very widely used commercially for data processing and for information storage and retrieval. Manufacturing industry has been affected by developments such as

Andreas Sofroniou

computer-integrated manufacture, and robotics.

Much scientific research has been transformed by the ability to analyse large quantities of numerical data and by the use of simulation techniques to model complex systems such as nuclear reactors and the weather. Many technical advances, such as space travel and advanced aircraft design, would have been impossible without the processing ability of computers.

Digital computers are available in a very wide range of powers, sizes, and costs, suitable for different applications. Advances in technology have led to rapid improvements in the performance of all types of computer systems: many personal computers are now more powerful than much larger, mainframe computers of the 1960s.

17

Configuration of a computer

A computer system can be regarded as being organized in a number of layers. The lowest layer is the hardware (the physical components of the system, as opposed to the software, the programs and other operating information used by the computer).

Both the information which is being processed (the data) and the processing instructions (the program) are stored in the form of bits of information in a memory. The memory unit is connected by a bus to the central processing unit (CPU), which is the other essential hardware component. The CPU takes one instruction at a time from the memory, decodes it, and then performs the action specified by the instruction.

Each instruction specifies a very simple operation, for example, multiplying together two numbers or checking that two pieces of information are identical.

Other hardware items are peripheral devices, which include permanent data storage devices such as hard and floppy disks, input devices for feeding information into the system, and output devices through which results are fed out.

A small layer of software above the hardware, called the microcode, allows the computer to execute a larger set of instructions than could be easily provided in hardware alone. The hardware and the microcode together execute machine code.

The next layer in the computer's organization is a much larger body of software, the operating system. It interprets additional, very complex instructions which allow reading from and writing to files, input devices, and output devices.

The layer above this is provided by the compiler or interpreter, which allows a programmer to write programs in a problem-orientated computer language, rather than in machine code or assembly language. The programmer working with such a language needs to know nothing of the layers below, so that a FORTRAN programmer can regard any computer with a FORTRAN compiler as if it were with a FORTRAN machine.

The final layer of software comprises the computer's applications programs. Computing is about the correct design and implementation of useful applications programs from a given specification. Techniques of software engineering are being developed which make specification, design, and implementation a less error-prone process.

Mathematics and formal reasoning are used to prove logically that the implementation of

Andreas Sofroniou

computer systems correspond to their specifications. Improving the reliability of programs is increasingly important as their use in safety-critical situations grows.

Some large computer programs have many millions of instructions, each instruction being a separate 'working part' that must function correctly. On this basis, computer programs are the most complex artefacts built by humans.

The major challenges for the future of computing and the programs are the development of software engineering techniques, very high-level computer languages, instant parallel processing, Internaut surfacing, cybernetics, and artificial intelligence.

TIME-CHART OF COMPUTING HISTORY

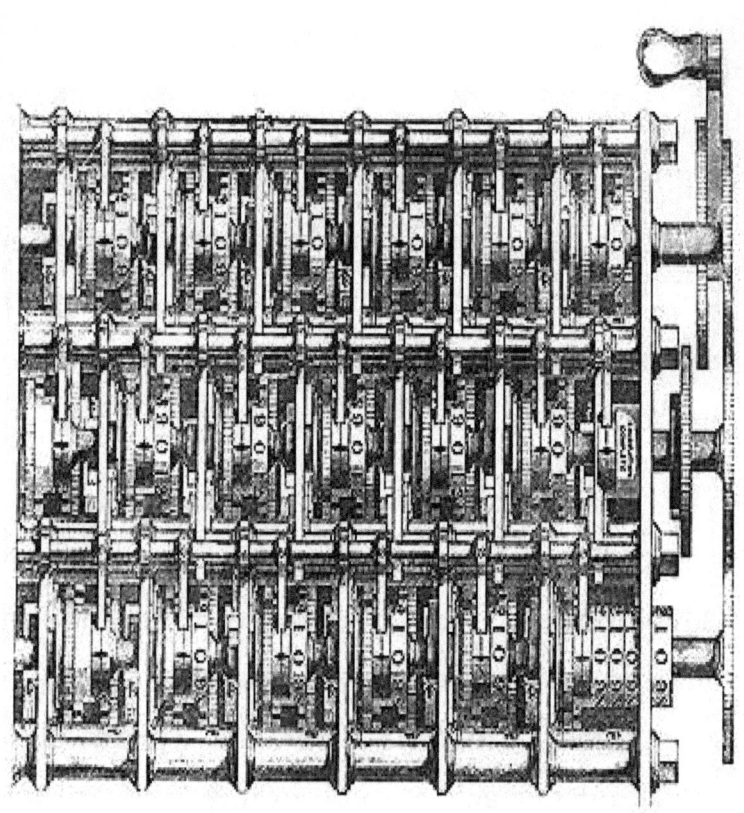

Difference Engine, 1835

Charles Babbage's difference engine no. 1.

Andreas Sofroniou

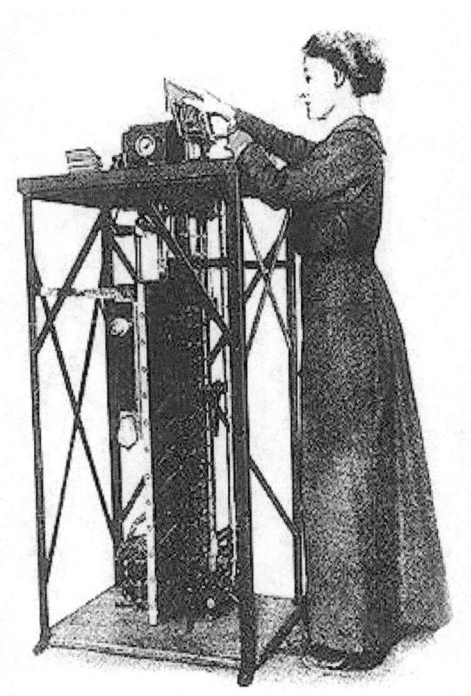

Hollerith 1890s.

Punch cards being made by early computer operator for the US Census, according to a system developed by H. Hollerith in the 1890s.

Andreas Sofroniou

ENIAC, 1946

A 1946 photo shows some of ENIAC's 18,000 tubes. ENIAC was one of the first electronic computing machines.

Andreas Sofroniou

BINAC, 1949

J. Presper Eckert, Jr., co-designer and James R. Weiner, chief engineer, look over the new portable 'Electronic Brain,' which can solve problems never before attempted by man.

The computer, called BINAC and developed in 1949, calculates 12,000 times faster than a human being, can compose music, and even plays chess. It was developed by Eckert and Dr. John W. Mauchley.

- 1950–1 J. Lyons and Co. install LEO, first commercial data handling computer, based on EDSAC computer designed at Cambridge University, UK.

Univac, 1951

Professor J. Eckert working on Univac, an early computer, (June 1951).

- **1954 UNIVAC I, the first commercial stored-program computer, marketed in USA.**

- **1956 IBM mass-produced the 701, their first commercial computer.**

IBM computer and attendant.

- **1959 First compiler developed for FORTRAN I.**

- **1963 First monolithic integrated circuits made, by Texas Instruments, USA.**

- **1971 The Atlas, the first modern mainframe computer, marketed commercially.**

- **1975 First microprocessor, the Intel 4004, marketed by the Intel Corporation, USA.**

- **1976 Introduction by Bell Laboratories of UNIX, the first widely adopted operating system.**

- **1977 The Altair, the first personal computer, marketed by MITS, USA.**

- **1978 Launch of the Cray-1, the first supercomputer.**

28

- Early 1980s Reports from Sweden, Italy, and Canada of eye strain and other health problems connected with use of VDU screens.

- 1981 Development by UK company INMOS of the transputer, a high-performance microcomputer in which both the processor and some memory are on the same chip.

- 1984 Reduced Instruction Set (RISC) microchip introduced. Enables computers to work ten times faster than previously possible.

- 1988 IBM personal computer introduced: lead to widespread use of personal computers in business.

- 1989 Apple Mackintosh marketed: uses a mouse and menus for standard procedures, rather than keyboard.

COMPUTER-AIDED SYSTEMS

Computer-aided design (CAD)

CAD is for the use of computer systems in engineering and desk-top publishing, for example to support the design of products. CAD complements the traditional design process, making it faster and more flexible, by providing an electronic drawing board for a design incorporating the required specifications. It usually employs a visual display unit and input devices such as enhanced keyboards and graphics pads.

CAD systems typically use software libraries of previous designs and commonly used components, which can be included by the designer in the new specification. Sometimes simulation can be used to test the feasibility of several alternative designs without

30

requiring them to be manufactured. The final design can then be plotted out as an engineering drawing or used in software to provide numerical control for machine-tools·

Computer-aided manufacture (CAM)

CAM is for the use of computer-based systems to control the machinery in manufacturing processes. CAM is an extension of computer-aided design (CAD); CAM systems usually make use of detailed databases produced by CAD systems. The databases (obtained either directly via a computer link, or from engineering drawings) are used to control machine-tool operation.

Most engineered components require many machining operations to be carried out sequentially; CAD data must therefore be adapted to control each machine-tool. Complexes of numerically controlled machine-tools and handling equipment such as transfer machines form flexible manufacturing systems. CAM is advantageous particularly where a range of slightly different products is required, since changes can be implemented simply by modifying the software.

Robotics represents an extension of CAM, where a general-purpose machine can be programmed for a variety of different tasks. A further development has been computer-integrated manufacture, the integration of design and production with other disciplines such as planning, purchasing, and financial control.

Computer-integrated manufacture (CIM)

CIM is for the integration of design and production aspects of manufacturing with traditionally separate areas such as planning, purchasing, data processing, financial control, and management support. CIM has evolved out of earlier techniques such as computer-aided design (CAD), computer-aided manufacture (CAM), numerical control of machine-tools, robotics, flexible manufacturing systems (FMS), and automated materials handling, all of which have been made possible by the use of information technology and computer-based systems.

As a result of the programmability and flexibility of the constituent processes, a CIM system can more easily be directed towards optimizing the effectiveness of the manufacturing operation as a whole, whereas earlier approaches to manufacturing often had to concentrate on maintaining or improving the efficiency of individual aspects only.

COMPUTER ARCHITECTURE

Hardware components

This refers to the design and structure of the hardware components of computer systems. The term embraces general considerations, such as whether a system is based on serial, parallel, or distributed computing, in which several computers are linked together.

It also covers more detailed aspects, such as a description of the internal structure of a central processing unit (CPU).

A micro-computer is often described as having an 8-bit, 16-bit, or 32-bit architecture according to the length of data word that can be processed by the CPU and the width of the data bus.

Andreas Sofroniou

Computer parts and peripherals

Part or Peripheral Name

- **arithmetic and logic unit (ALU)**
- **bar-code reader**
- **buffer**
- **bus**
- **cache memory**
- **cartridge**
- **cassette**
- **CD-ROM**
- **console**
- **central processing unit (CPU)**
- **control unit**
- **digitizer**
- **disk**
- **diskette**
- **dynamic RAM (DRAM)**
- **drum scanner**

Andreas Sofroniou

- dynamic memory
- erasable programmable read-only me (EPROM)
- fax modem
- firmware
- fixed disk
- flash memory
- flat-bed plotter
- flat-bed scanner
- floppy disk
- hard disk
- hardware
- input-output device
- input-output port
- joystick
- keyboard
- light-pen
- magnetic-tape unit (MTU)
- main memory
- mathematics coprocessor

Andreas Sofroniou

- memory
- microfloppy
- microprocessor
- minidisk/minidiskette
- modem
- monitor
- mouse
- non-volatile memory
- optical disk
- plotter
- port
- primary memory
- printer
- processor
- random access memory (RAM)
- register
- read only memory (ROM)
- removable disk
- scanner
- secondary memory

Andreas Sofroniou

- **semiconductor memory**
- **software**
- **solid-state memory**
- **static RAM (SRAM)**
- **tape streamer**
- **terminal**
- **trackerball**
- **visual display unit (VDU)**
- **voice synthesizer**
- **wand**
- **Winchester disk**

Digital and analogue computers

A computer configuration is a device for storing and processing data, according to a program of instructions stored within the computer itself. The term computer normally refers to electronic digital computers, but analogue computers also exist for use in specialist applications.

Computers are 'universal' information-processing machines: any information-processing task that can be specified by an algorithm (a well-defined sequence of instructions) can, in principle, be performed by a computer. Unlike most other machines, it is not necessary to build a new computer for each new task.

Computers can therefore perform a very large number of useful tasks, although limits do exist: it can be proved that some problems are incomputable. The mathematical study of

39

what tasks are capable of being computed is known as compatibility, and complexity is the study of how hard it is to compute a task. Numerical analysis concerns the fastest and most accurate way to solve numerical problems.

The digital computer is one of the most significant innovations of the 20th century (see computer, history of). In the four decades since its introduction it has had an impact on almost all areas of human.

Computers are very widely used commercially for data processing and for information storage and retrieval. Manufacturing industry has been affected by developments such as computer-integrated manufacture, and robotics. Much scientific research has been transformed by the ability to analyse large quantities of numerical data and by the use of simulation techniques to model complex

Andreas Sofroniou

systems such as nuclear reactors and the weather.

Many technical advances, such as space travel and advanced aircraft design, would have been impossible without the processing ability of computers. Digital computers are available in a very wide range of powers, sizes, and costs, suitable for different applications. Advances in technology have led to rapid improvements in the performance of all types of computer systems: many personal computers are now more powerful than much larger, mainframe computers of the 1960s.

A computer system can be regarded as being organized in a number of layers. The lowest layer is the hardware (the physical components of the system, as opposed to the software, the programs and other operating information used by the computer). Both the information which is being processed (the data) and the processing instructions (the program) are stored in the form of bits of information in a memory.

The memory unit is connected by a bus to the central processing unit (CPU), which is the other essential hardware component. The CPU takes one instruction at a time from the memory, decodes it, and then performs the action specified by the instruction. Each instruction specifies a very simple operation, for example, multiplying together two numbers or checking that two pieces of information are identical.

Other hardware items are peripheral devices, which include permanent data storage devices such as hard and floppy disks, input devices for feeding information into the system, and output devices through which results are fed out. A small layer of software above the hardware, called the microcode, allows the computer to execute a larger set of instructions than could be easily provided in hardware alone. The hardware and the microcode together execute machine code.

The next layer in the computer's organization is a much larger body of software, the operating system. It interprets additional, very complex instructions which allow reading from and writing to files, input devices, and output devices. The layer above this is provided by the compiler or interpreter, which allows a programmer to write programs in a problem-orientated computer language, rather than in machine code or assembly language. The programmer working with such a language needs to know nothing of the layers below, so that a FORTRAN programmer can regard any computer with a FORTRAN compiler as if it were with a FORTRAN machine.

The final layer of software comprises the computer's applications programs. Computing is

43

about the correct design and implementation of useful applications programs from a given specification.

Techniques of software engineering are being developed which make specification, design, and implementation a less error-prone process. Mathematics and formal reasoning are used to prove logically that the implementation of computer systems correspond to their specifications. Improving the reliability of programs is increasingly important as their use in safety-critical situations grows.

Some large computer programs have many millions of instructions, each instruction being a separate 'working part' that must function correctly. On this basis, computer programs are the most complex artefacts built by humans. The major challenges of computing in the future are the development of software engineering techniques, very high-level computer languages, and parallel processing.

Important high-level computer languages

<u>Language</u>   <u>Description</u>

ADA   Specifically developed for the U.S.
Department of Defense to standardize
programming operations. Increasingly
used on large computer systems,
especially those in military
applications.

ALGOL,   ALGOrithmic language, designed by IBM
and favoured by professional programmers
for its formality and structure.

ALGOL-68   ALGOL languages have never
                attracted widespread popularity,
                but are still occasionally used
                for specific applications.

BASIC   Beginner's   All-purpose
                Symbolic Instruction Code.
                Designed to be easily learnt and
                useful for general
                programming applications.
                Very popular despite its
                limitations.

C   An efficient language created by
                Bell Laboratories. Because, in
                some applications, it compares
                favourably
                in speed of execution with lower
                level languages like assembly
                language, C is now widely used
                by professional

programmers, especially in system programs and personal computers.

COBOL   COmmon Business-Oriented Language. Widely used on mainframe systems in business applications, where its

English-like syntax makes it easy to understand.

FORTRAN   FORmula TRANslator. Developed for programming of scientific, mathematical, and engineering calculations.

Released commercially in 1957, it is widely used, especially on mainframe and minicomputer systems.

LISP   LISt Processing language,

47

produced in 1959 to simplify the processing of lists of separate but related items.

Also used in artificial intelligence applications, including fifth-generation computer design.

Pascal   A descendent of ALGOL, specifically designed to encourage good programming practice. Has become popular in professional computing communities.

PROLOG   Developed by the University of Marseilles, France, for artificial intelligence applications. Now used in fifth-generation computer design.

Computer programs

Computer language, a specialized, formal language used to write computer programs.

Computer languages were developed to relieve programmers of the arduous task of writing programs directly in machine code.

There are two broad classes of conventional programming languages:

- Low-level languages, such as assembly language, in which each instruction represents a single machine code operation, and

- High-level languages, in which each instruction may represent an operation involving many machine code instructions.

49

In both cases a special program, either an assembler, a compiler, or an interpreter, must be used to translate the source code to machine code before the program can be run on a computer.

A job-control language, or command language, is the usual interface between a computer and the operating system. It allows the user to describe what tasks, or jobs, are to be processed by the computer.

The system interprets the user's commands and runs the required application programs.

The Swiss engineer Konrad Zuse is credited with the invention of the first programming language shortly after World War II.

Autocode

The Autocode is the first high-level language complete with translation program, and was developed at Manchester University, UK, in the early 1950s.

Since then hundreds of different programming languages have been designed, but only a few are in widespread use. The first two languages to be widely used (FORTRAN and COBOL) were released around 1957.

Both languages dominated their respective fields for the next two decades and are still in widespread use. In 1958 ALGOL was developed by an international committee.

Although ALGOL evolved over the next decade it had greater theoretical than practical significance.

Andreas Sofroniou

However, it did spawn PASCAL, one of today's most commonly used languages. BASIC, which was developed in the mid-1960s at Dartmouth College, USA, is the best-known language for programming microcomputers.

Nowadays, the preferred language for much professional program development is C, designed at Bell Laboratories, USA, in 1971 to implement the UNIX operating system.

Most artificial intelligence applications use symbolic or logical languages, such as LISP and PROLOG, rather than conventional programming languages.

Andreas Sofroniou

PROGRAMMING LANGUAGES

(Education-oriented, Algorithmic and Business-oriented)

The most popular of these languages are listed alphabetically below:

Ada

Ada was named for Augusta Ada King, countess of Lovelace, who was an assistant to the 19th-century English inventor Charles Babbage, and is sometimes called the first computer programmer. Ada, the language, was developed in the early 1980s for the U.S. Department of Defense for large-scale programming. It combined Pascal-like notation with the ability to package operations and data into independent modules.

Its first form, Ada 83, was not fully object-oriented, but the subsequent Ada 95 provided objects and the ability to construct hierarchies of them. While no longer mandated for use in work for the Department of Defense, Ada remains an effective language for engineering large programs.

ALGOL

ALGOL (algorithmic language) was designed by a committee of American and European computer scientists during 1958–60 for publishing algorithms, as well as for doing computations. Like LISP (described in the next section), ALGOL had recursive subprograms—procedures that could invoke themselves to solve a problem by reducing it to a smaller problem of the same kind.

ALGOL introduced block structure, in which a program is composed of blocks that might contain both data and instructions and have the same structure as an entire program. Block structure became a powerful tool for building large programs out of small components.

ALGOL contributed a notation for describing the structure of a programming language, Backus–Naur Form, which in some variation became the standard tool for stating the syntax (grammar) of programming languages. ALGOL was widely used in Europe, and for many years it remained the language in which computer algorithms were published. Many important languages, such as Pascal and Ada (both described later), are its descendants.

BASIC

BASIC (beginner's all-purpose symbolic instruction code) was designed at Dartmouth College in the mid-1960s by John Kemeny and Thomas Kurtz. It was intended to be easy to learn by novices, particularly non-computer science majors, and to run well on a time-sharing computer with many users. It had simple data structures and notation and it was interpreted: a BASIC program was translated line-by-line and executed as it was translated, which made it easy to locate programming errors.

Its small size and simplicity also made BASIC a popular language for early personal computers. Its recent forms have adopted many of the data and control structures of other contemporary languages, which makes it more powerful but less convenient for beginners.

C

The C programming language was developed in 1972 by Dennis Ritchie and Brian

Kernighan at the AT&T Corporation for programming computer operating systems. Its capacity to structure data and programs through the composition of smaller units is comparable to that of ALGOL.

It uses a compact notation and provides the programmer with the ability to operate with the addresses of data as well as with their values. This ability is important in systems programming, and C shares with assembly language the power to exploit all the features of a computer's internal architecture. C, along with its descendant C++, remains one of the most common languages.

C++

The C++ language, developed by Bjarne Stroustrup at AT&T in the mid-1980s, extended C by adding objects to it while preserving the efficiency of C programs. It has been one of the most important languages for both education and industrial programming.

Large parts of many operating systems, such as the Microsoft Corporation's Windows 98, were written in C++.

COBOL

COBOL (common business oriented language) has been heavily used by businesses since its inception in 1959. A committee of computer manufacturers and users and U.S. government organizations established CODASYL (Committee on Data Systems and Languages) to develop and oversee the language standard in order to ensure its portability across diverse systems.

COBOL uses an English-like notation—novel when introduced. Business computations organize and manipulate large quantities of data, and COBOL introduced the record data structure for such tasks. A record clusters heterogeneous data such as a name, ID number, age, and address into a single unit. This contrasts with scientific languages, in which homogeneous arrays of numbers are common. Records are an important example of "chunking" data into a single object, and they appear in nearly all modern languages.

FORTRAN, *Formula Translation*

This computer-programming language was created in 1957 by John Backus that shortened the process of programming and made computer programming more accessible.

The creation of FORTRAN, which debuted in 1957, marked a significant stage in the development of computer-programming languages. Previous programming was written in machine (first-generation) language or assembly (second-generation) language, which required the programmer to write instructions in binary or hexadecimal arithmetic.

Frustration with the arduous nature of such programming led Backus to search for a simpler, more accessible way to communicate with computers. During the three-year development stage, Backus led an eclectic team of 10 International Business Machines (IBM) employees to create a language that combined a form of English shorthand with algebraic equations.

FORTRAN enabled the rapid writing of computer programs that ran nearly as efficiently as programs that had been laboriously hand coded in machine language. As computers were rare and extremely expensive, inefficient programs were a greater financial problem than the lengthy and painstaking development of machine-language programs.

With the creation of an efficient higher-level (or natural) language, also known as a third-generation language, computer programming moved beyond a small coterie to include engineers and scientists, who were instrumental in expanding the use of computers.

By allowing the creation of natural-language programs that ran as efficiently as hand-coded ones, FORTRAN became the programming language of choice in the late 1950s.

It was updated a number of times in the 1950s and 1960s in order to remain competitive with more contemporary programming languages. FORTRAN 77 was released in 1978, followed by FORTRAN 90 in 1991 and further updates in 1996 and 2004. However, fourth- and fifth-generation languages largely supplanted FORTRAN outside academic circles beginning in the 1970s.

Hypertalk

Hypertalk was designed as "programming for the rest of us" by Bill Atkinson for Apple's Macintosh. Using a simple English-like syntax, Hypertalk enabled anyone to combine text, graphics, and audio quickly into "linked stacks" that could be navigated by clicking with a mouse on standard buttons supplied by the program.

Hypertalk was particularly popular among educators in the 1980s and early '90s for classroom multimedia presentations. Although Hypertalk had many features of object-oriented languages (described in the next section), Apple did not develop it for other computer platforms and let it languish;

as Apple's market share declined in the 1990s, a new cross-platform way of displaying multimedia left Hypertalk all but obsolete

Java

In the early 1990s, Java was designed by Sun Microsystems, Inc., as a programming language for the World Wide Web (WWW). Although it resembled C++ in appearance, it was fully object-oriented. In particular, Java dispensed with lower-level features, including the ability to manipulate data addresses, a capability that is neither desirable nor useful in programs for distributed systems.

In order to be portable, Java programs are translated by a Java Virtual Machine specific to each computer platform, which then executes the Java program. In addition to adding interactive capabilities to the Internet through Web "applets," Java has been widely used for programming small and portable devices, such as mobile telephones.

LISP

LISP (list processing) was developed about 1960 by John McCarthy at the Massachusetts Institute of Technology (MIT) and was founded on the mathematical theory of recursive functions (in which a function appears in its own definition).

A LISP program is a function applied to data, rather than being a sequence of procedural steps as in FORTRAN and ALGOL. LISP uses a very simple notation in which operations and their operands are given in a parenthesized list. For example, (+ a (* b c)) stands for $a + b*c$. Although this appears awkward, the notation works well for computers. LISP also uses the list structure to represent data, and, because programs and data use the same structure, it is easy for a LISP program to operate on other programs as data.

LISP became a common language for artificial intelligence (AI) programming, partly owing to the confluence of LISP and AI work at MIT and partly because AI programs capable of "learning" could be written in LISP as self-modifying programs. LISP has evolved through numerous dialects, such as Scheme and Common LISP.

Logo

Logo originated in the late 1960s as a simplified LISP dialect for education; Seymour Papert and others used it at MIT to teach mathematical thinking to schoolchildren. It had a more conventional syntax than LISP and featured "turtle graphics," a simple method for generating computer graphics. (The name came from an early project to program a turtlelike robot.)

Turtle graphics used body-centred instructions, in which an object was moved around a screen by commands, such as "left 90" and "forward," that specified actions relative to the current position and orientation of the object rather than in terms of a fixed framework. Together with recursive routines, this technique made it easy to program intricate and attractive patterns.

Object-oriented languages

Object-oriented languages help to manage complexity in large programs. Objects package data and the operations on them so that only the operations are publicly accessible and internal details of the data structures are hidden.

This information hiding made large-scale programming easier by allowing a programmer to think about each part of the program in isolation. In addition, objects may be derived from more general ones, "inheriting" their capabilities. Such an object hierarchy made it possible to define specialized objects without repeating all that is in the more general ones.

Object-oriented programming began with the Simula language (1967), which added information hiding to ALGOL. Another influential object-oriented language was Smalltalk (1980), in which a program was a set of objects that interacted by sending messages to one another.

Pascal

About 1970 Niklaus Wirth of Switzerland designed Pascal to teach structured

Andreas Sofroniou

programming, which emphasized the orderly use of conditional and loop control structures without GOTO statements.

Although Pascal resembled ALGOL in notation, it provided the ability to define data types with which to organize complex information, a feature beyond the capabilities of ALGOL as well as FORTRAN and COBOL. User-defined data types allowed the programmer to introduce names for complex data, which the language translator could then check for correct usage before running a program.

During the late 1970s and '80s, Pascal was one of the most widely used languages for programming instruction. It was available on nearly all computers, and, because of its familiarity, clarity, and security, it was used for production software as well as for education.

Andreas Sofroniou

SQL

SQL (structured query language) is a language for specifying the organization of databases (collections of records). Databases organized with SQL are called relational because SQL provides the ability to query a database for information that falls in a given relation.

For example, a query might be "find all records with both last_name Smith and city New York." Commercial database programs commonly use a SQL-like language for their queries.

Visual Basic

Visual Basic was developed by Microsoft to extend the capabilities of BASIC by adding objects and "event-driven" programming:

buttons, menus, and other elements of graphical user interfaces (GUIs). Visual Basic can also be used within other Microsoft software to program small routines.

Declarative languages

Declarative languages, also called nonprocedural or very high level, are programming languages in which (ideally) a program specifies what is to be done rather than how to do it. In such languages there is less difference between the specification of a program and its implementation than in the procedural languages described so far. The two common kinds of declarative languages are logic and functional languages.

Logic programming languages, of which PROLOG (programming in logic) is the best known, state a program as a set of logical relations (e.g., a grandparent is the parent of a parent of someone). Such languages are similar to the SQL database language. A program is executed by an "inference engine" that answers a query by searching these relations systematically to make inferences that will answer a query. PROLOG has been used extensively in natural language processing and other AI programs.

Functional languages have a mathematical style. A functional program is constructed by applying functions to arguments. Functional languages, such as LISP, ML, and Haskell, are used as research tools in language development, in automated mathematical theorem provers, and in some commercial projects.

Scripting languages

Scripting languages are sometimes called little languages. They are intended to solve relatively small programming problems that do not require the overhead of data declarations and other features needed to make large programs manageable.

Scripting languages are used for writing operating system utilities, for special-purpose file-manipulation programs, and, because they are easy to learn, sometimes for considerably larger programs.

PERL (practical extraction and report language) was developed in the late 1980s, originally for use with the UNIX operating system. It was intended to have all the capabilities of earlier scripting languages. PERL provided many ways to state common operations and thereby allowed a programmer to adopt any convenient style.

In the 1990s it became popular as a system-programming tool, both for small utility programs and for prototypes of larger ones. Together with other languages discussed below, it also became popular for programming computer Web "servers."

Document formatting languages

Document formatting languages specify the organization of printed text and graphics. They fall into several classes: text formatting notation that can serve the same functions as a word processing program, page description languages that are interpreted by a printing device and, most generally, mark-up languages that describe the intended function of portions of a document.

TeX

TeX was developed during 1977–86 as a text formatting language by Donald Knuth, a Stanford University professor, to improve the quality of mathematical notation in his books. Text formatting systems, unlike WYSIWYG ("What You See Is What You Get") word processors, embed plain text formatting commands in a document, which are then interpreted by the language processor to produce a formatted document for display or printing. TeX marks italic text, for example, as {\it this is italicized}, which is then displayed as this is italicized.

TeX largely replaced earlier text formatting languages. Its powerful and flexible abilities gave an expert precise control over such things as the choice of fonts, layout of tables, mathematical notation, and the inclusion of graphics within a document.

It is generally used with the aid of "macro" packages that define simple commands for common operations, such as starting a new paragraph; LaTeX is a widely used package. TeX contains numerous standard "style sheets" for different types of documents, and these may be further adapted by each user.

There are also related programs such as BibTeX, which manages bibliographies and has style sheets for all of the common bibliography styles, and versions of TeX for languages with various alphabets.

PostScript

PostScript is a page-description language developed in the early 1980s by Adobe Systems Incorporated on the basis of work at Xerox PARC (Palo Alto Research Center). Such languages describe documents in terms that can be interpreted by a personal computer to display the document on its screen or by a microprocessor in a printer or a typesetting device.

PostScript commands can, for example, precisely position text, in various fonts and sizes, draw images that are mathematically described, and specify colour or shading. PostScript uses postfix, also called reverse Polish notation, in which an operation name follows its arguments.

Thus, "300 600 20 270 arc stroke" means: draw ("stroke") a 270-degree arc with radius 20 at location (300, 600). Although PostScript can be read and written by a programmer, it is normally produced by text formatting programs, word processors, or graphic display tools.

The success of PostScript is due to its specification's being in the public domain and to its being a good match for high-resolution laser printers. It has influenced the development of printing fonts, and manufacturers produce a large variety of PostScript fonts.

SGML

SGML (standard generalized markup language) is an international standard for the definition of markup languages; that is, it is a metalanguage. Markup consists of notations called tags that specify the function of a piece of text or how it is to be displayed. SGML emphasizes descriptive markup, in which a tag might be "<emphasis>." Such a markup denotes the document function, and it could be interpreted as reverse video on a computer screen, underlining by a typewriter, or italics in typeset text.

SGML is used to specify DTDs (document type definitions). A DTD defines a kind of document, such as a report, by specifying what elements must appear in the document—e.g., <Title>—and giving rules for the use of document elements, such as that a paragraph may appear within a table entry but a table may not appear within a paragraph.

A marked-up text may be analyzed by a parsing program to determine if it conforms to a DTD. Another program may read the markups to prepare an index or to translate the document into PostScript for printing. Yet another might generate large type or audio for readers with visual or hearing disabilities.

Other languages

Various other languages developed over the years and not frequently used are:

APL, B, BCPL, COMAL, CORAL, CPL, Forth, JOVIAL, Modula, PL/1, POP, SIMULA, SNOBOL.

WORLD WIDE WEB DISPLAY LANGUAGES

Surfing in cyberspace

HTML

The World Wide Web is a system for displaying text, graphics, and audio retrieved over the Internet on a computer monitor. Each

Andreas Sofroniou

retrieval unit is known as a Web page, and such pages frequently contain "links" that allow related pages to be retrieved. HTML (hypertext mark-up language) is the mark-up language for encoding Web pages. It was designed by Tim Berners-Lee at the CERN nuclear physics laboratory in Switzerland during the 1980s and is defined by an SGML DTD. HTML mark-up tags specify document elements such as headings, paragraphs, and tables.

They mark up a document for display by a computer program known as a Web browser. The browser interprets the tags, displaying the headings, paragraphs, and tables in a layout that is adapted to the screen size and fonts available to it.

XML

HTML does not allow one to define new text elements; that is, it is not extensible. XML (extensible markup language) is a simplified form of SGML intended for documents that are published on the Web. Like SGML, XML uses DTDs to define document types and the meanings of tags used in them.

XML adopts conventions that make it easy to parse, such as that document entities are marked by both a beginning and an ending tag, such as <BEGIN>...</BEGIN>. XML provides more kinds of hypertext links than HTML, such as bidirectional links and links relative to a document subsection.

Because an author may define new tags, an XML DTD must also contain rules that instruct a Web browser how to interpret them—how an entity is to be displayed or how it is to generate an action such as preparing an e-mail message.

Web scripting

Web pages marked up with HTML or XML are largely static documents. Web scripting can add information to a page as a reader uses it or let the reader enter information that may, for example, be passed on to the order department of an online business. CGI (common gateway interface) provides one mechanism; it transmits requests and responses between the reader's Web browser and the Web server that provides the page.

The CGI component on the server contains small programs called scripts that take information from the browser system or provide it for display. A simple script might ask the reader's name; determine the Internet address of the system that the reader uses, and print a greeting. Scripts may be written in any programming language, but, because they are generally simple text-processing routines, scripting languages like PERL are particularly appropriate.

Another approach is to use a language designed for Web scripts to be executed by the browser. JavaScript is one such language, designed by the Netscape Communications Corp., which may be used with both Netscape's and Microsoft's browsers.

JavaScript is a simple language, quite different from Java. A JavaScript program may be embedded in a Web page with the HTML tag <script language="JavaScript">. JavaScript instructions following that tag will be executed by the browser when the page is selected. In order to speed up display of dynamic (interactive) pages, JavaScript is often combined with XML or some other language for exchanging information between the server and the client's browser.

In particular, the XMLHttpRequest command enables asynchronous data requests from the server without requiring the server to resend the entire Web page. This approach, or "philosophy," of programming is called Ajax (asynchronous JavaScript and XML).

Visual Basic

VB Script is a subset of Visual Basic. Originally developed for Microsoft's Office suite of programs, it was later used for Web scripting as well. Its capabilities are similar to those of JavaScript, and it may be embedded in HTML in the same fashion.

Behind the use of such scripting languages for Web programming lies the idea of component programming, in which programs are constructed by combining independent previously written components without any further language processing. JavaScript and VB Script programs were designed as components that may be attached to Web browsers to control how they display information.

ELEMENTS OF PROGRAMMING

Structures

Despite notational differences, contemporary computer languages provide many of the same programming structures. These include basic control structures and data structures. The former provide the means to express algorithms, and the latter provide ways to organize information.

Algorithmic languages are designed to express mathematical or symbolic computations. They can express algebraic operations in notation similar to mathematics and allow the use of subprograms that package commonly used operations for reuse. They were the first high-level languages.

86

Compiler

The compiler is a computer program that translates high-level computer languages, such as FORTRAN, ALGOL, and C, into machine code that can be executed directly on the computer. Unlike an interpreter, a compiler converts the whole program into machine code before running it, which is frequently more efficient.

Machine code

Machine code is the binary code used to represent the instructions that a computer executes. It represents the lowest possible level at which a computer can be programmed. Any program written in a high-level computer language or assembly language must be translated into machine code before it can be executed.

Andreas Sofroniou

Transputer

The transputer is a chip that incorporates all the functions of a microprocessor, including memory. Transputers have in-built communications links so that they can easily be linked to similar processors to form parallel processing systems. Transputers can divide up tasks between several identical processors, enabling them to handle large amounts of data very quickly. Conventional serial computers carry out tasks serially using one very fast processor. The transputer was built in 1978 by Inmos in the UK.

The programming language designed for the transputer is occam, a computer language based upon the concept of parallel execution. It can provide automatic communication and co-ordination between concurrent processes. Arrays of Transputers are used to run applications where a significant increase in speed over conventional computers is required.

Program (in computing)

This is a set of coded instructions (the software) to control the operation of a computer or other machine. For example, utility programs perform tasks usually related to the operating system.

Since the central processing unit only processes machine code, programs written in a high-level computer language or assembly language must be translated into machine code before execution.

Assembly language

Assembly is a computer language that represents machine code programs in a form people can read. Each machine code instruction is represented by a short mnemonic code. Memory registers and storage addresses may be referred to by symbolic names rather than numeric codes, and labels and comments can be used to improve legibility.

Assembly language programs have to be translated into machine code by a special program called an assembler before they can be run on the computer. Because an assembly language represents machine code instructions directly, it is specific to a particular type of central processing unit.

Operating system

This is the software that manages the resources of a computer system, independent of the use to which the computer is put.

In addition to controlling the operation of hardware, the operating system also manages the transmission of data to and from memory, the disk drives, and peripherals such as keyboards, displays, and printers.

Widely used operating systems include MS-DOS (MicroSoft Disk Operating System), OS/2, and UNIX.

Andreas Sofroniou

ARTIFICIAL INTELLIGENCE (AI)

Intelligence

AI is considered to be 'the science of making machines do things that would require intelligence if done by humans' as defined in 1968 by Marvin Minsky of the Massachusetts Institute of Technology, USA. Sensing, reasoning, pattern recognition, speech recognition, and problem-solving are among such tasks.

The degree of sophistication that constitutes AI tends to be revised upwards with each new generation of computers.

At its most ambitious level AI has the goal of creating computers and robots capable of reproducing a broad range of human behaviour.

Andreas Sofroniou

Doubts remain, however, about whether such systems are theoretically or practically possible, because of the vast complexity of the human brain. Unlike the human brain, most computers act serially, one operation at a time.

Even supercomputers developed in the 1980s that use 'parallel processing' to carry out billions of operations per second barely begin to match human brain capacity.

Moreover, it has been argued that the brain does not operate using computable algorithms. Experiments in machine translation of natural languages in the 1960s revealed the 'frame problem': most human thought processes use huge amounts of background knowledge or 'context' which it is very difficult to duplicate in a computer.

However, one important result of AI research is the development of systems known as neural networks, which can be 'taught' to solve problems.

These show promise for a number of different AI applications, particularly those involving pattern recognition.

The demands of AI have also stimulated the development of computer languages, such as PROLOG and LISP, which are better suited to represent and process symbolic structures than more conventional languages.

'Pseudo-intelligence' is one term for computer applications being developed in translation systems, semi-automatic offices in which human speech and instructions are turned into a properly laid-out document, in linguistic and psycholinguistic studies, and in robotics-
-replacing human actions by those of a robot, on the production line or in an artificial limb, for example.

93

Robot sensing is used in weapons guidance systems and in product quality control. The impact of such developments is likely to be huge.

Most approaches to AI require powerful computer hardware, and it is only since the early 1980s that this has become sufficiently cost-effective to make practical applications possible.

Fifth-generation computers are being developed specifically for use in artificial intelligence. Expert systems were amongst the first AI techniques to be used in practical applications.

Fifth-generation computer

This is a term applied to computer systems currently being developed specifically to support artificial intelligence.

Andreas Sofroniou

In the early 1980s Japan set up a major research project intended to develop the computer hardware and software necessary to perform complex tasks such as machine translation of natural languages, speech recognition, and vision in robotics.

Similar projects were also started in the USA and Europe.

The use of artificial intelligence to solve practical problems requires very powerful computers and fifth-generation computers are likely to use more complex computer architectures than conventional computers, involving parallel processing.

In 1991 Japan began a new ten-year research initiative, replacing the fifth-generation programme, to investigate neural networks.

Andreas Sofroniou

WORLD WIDE WEB DISPLAY LANGUAGES

HTML

The World Wide Web is a system for displaying text, graphics, and audio retrieved over the Internet on a computer monitor. Each retrieval unit is known as a Web page, and such pages frequently contain "links" that allow related pages to be retrieved. HTML (hypertext markup language) is the markup language for encoding Web pages. It was designed by Tim Berners-Lee at the CERN nuclear physics laboratory in Switzerland during the 1980s and is defined by an SGML DTD. HTML mark-up tags specify document elements such as headings, paragraphs, and tables. They mark up a document for display by a computer program known as a Web browser. The browser interprets the tags, displaying the headings, paragraphs, and tables in a layout that is adapted to the screen size and fonts available to it.

HTML documents also contain anchors, which are tags that specify links to other Web pages. An anchor has the form <A HREF= "http://www.britannica.com"> Encyclopædia Britannica</A>, where the quoted string is the URL (universal resource locator) to which the link points (the Web "address") and the text following it is what appears in a Web browser, underlined to show that it is a link to another page. What is displayed as a single page may also be formed from multiple URLs, some containing text and others graphics.

XML

HTML does not allow one to define new text elements; that is, it is not extensible. XML (extensible markup language) is a simplified form of SGML intended for documents that are published on the Web. Like SGML, XML uses DTDs to define document types and the meanings of tags used in them. XML adopts conventions that make it easy to parse, such as that document entities are marked by both a beginning and an ending tag, such as <BEGIN>...</BEGIN>. XML provides more kinds of hypertext links than HTML, such as bidirectional links and links relative to a document subsection.

Because an author may define new tags, an XML DTD must also contain rules that instruct a Web browser how to interpret them—how an entity is to be displayed or how it is to generate an action such as preparing an e-mail message.

Web scripting

Web pages marked up with HTML or XML are largely static documents. Web scripting can add information to a page as a reader uses it or let the reader enter information that may, for example, be passed on to the order department of an online business. CGI (common gateway interface) provides one mechanism; it transmits requests and responses between the reader's Web browser and the Web server that provides the page. The CGI component on the server contains small programs called scripts that take information from the browser system or provide it for display. A simple script might ask the reader's name, determine the Internet address of the system that the reader uses, and print a greeting. Scripts may be written in any programming language, but, because they are generally simple text-processing routines, scripting languages like PERL are particularly appropriate.

Another approach is to use a language designed for Web scripts to be executed by the browser. JavaScript is one such language, designed by the Netscape Communications Corp., which may be used with both Netscape's and Microsoft's browsers. JavaScript is a simple language, quite different from Java. A JavaScript program may be embedded in a Web page with the HTML tag <script language="JavaScript">. JavaScript instructions following that tag will be executed by the browser when the page is selected. In order to speed up display of dynamic (interactive) pages, JavaScript is often combined with XML or some other language for exchanging information between the server and the client's browser. In particular, the XMLHttpRequest command enables asynchronous data requests from the server without requiring the server to resend the entire Web page. This approach, or "philosophy," of programming is called Ajax (*asynchronous JavaScript and XML*).

VB Script is a subset of Visual Basic. Originally developed for Microsoft's Office suite of programs, it was later used for Web scripting as well. Its capabilities are similar to those of JavaScript, and it may be embedded in HTML in the same fashion.

Behind the use of such scripting languages for Web programming lies the idea of component programming, in which programs are constructed by combining independent previously written components without any further language processing. JavaScript and VB Script programs were designed as components that may be attached to Web browsers to control how they display information.

Elements of programming

Despite notational differences, contemporary computer languages provide many of the

Andreas Sofroniou

same programming structures. These include basic control structures and data structures. The former provide the means to express algorithms, and the latter provide ways to organize information.

Control structures

Programs written in procedural languages, the most common kind, are like recipes, having lists of ingredients and step-by-step instructions for using them.

The three basic control structures in virtually every procedural language are:

1. Sequence—combine the liquid ingredients, and next add the dry ones.

2. Conditional—if the tomatoes are fresh then simmer them, but if canned, skip this step.

Andreas Sofroniou

3. Iterative—beat the egg whites until they form soft peaks.

Sequence is the default control structure; instructions are executed one after another. They might, for example, carry out a series of arithmetic operations, assigning results to variables, to find the roots of a quadratic equation $ax^2 + bx + c = 0$.

The conditional IF-THEN or IF-THEN-ELSE control structure allows a program to follow alternative paths of execution. Iteration, or looping, gives computers much of their power. They can repeat a sequence of steps as often as necessary and appropriate repetitions of quite simple steps can solve complex problems.

These control structures can be combined. A sequence may contain several loops; a loop may contain a loop nested within it, or the two branches of a conditional may each contain

Andreas Sofroniou

sequences with loops and more conditionals. In the "pseudocode" used in this article, "*" indicates multiplication and "←" is used to assign values to variables.

The following programming fragment employs the IF-THEN structure for finding one root of the quadratic equation, using the quadratic formula:

The quadratic formula assumes that *a* is nonzero and that the discriminant (the portion within the square root sign) is not negative (in order to obtain a real number root).

Conditionals check those assumptions:

- IF *a* = 0 THEN

- ROOT ← −*c*/*b*

- ELSE

Andreas Sofroniou

- DISCRIMINANT $\leftarrow$ $b^*b - 4^*a^*c$

- IF DISCRIMINANT ≥ 0 THEN

- ROOT $\leftarrow$ $(-b +$ SQUARE_ROOT(DISCRIMINANT))$/2$ $^*a$

- ENDIF

- ENDIF

The SQUARE_ROOT function used in the above fragment is an example of a subprogram (also called a procedure, subroutine, or function). A subprogram is like a sauce recipe given once and used as part of many other recipes. Subprograms take inputs (the quantity needed) and produce results (the sauce).

Commonly used subprograms are generally in a collection or library provided with a language. Subprograms may call other subprograms in their definitions, as shown by the following routine (where ABS is the absolute-value function).

SQUARE_ROOT is implemented by using a WHILE (indefinite) loop that produces a good approximation for the square root of real numbers unless x is very small or very large.

A subprogram is written by declaring its name, the type of input data, and the output:

- FUNCTION SQUARE_ROOT(REAL x) RETURNS REAL

- ROOT $\leftarrow$ 1.0

- WHILE ABS(ROOT*ROOT $-$ x) $\geq$ 0.000001

- AND WHILE ROOT $\leftarrow$ (x/ROOT + ROOT)/2

- RETURN ROOT

Subprograms can break a problem into smaller, more tractable sub-problems. Sometimes a problem may be solved by reducing it to a sub-problem that is a smaller version of the original.

In that case the routine is known as a recursive subprogram because it solves the problem by repeatedly calling itself.

For example, the factorial function in mathematics $(n! = n \cdot (n-1) \cdots 3 \cdot 2 \cdot 1$—i.e., the product of the first n integers), can be programmed as a recursive routine:

.   FUNCTION FACTORIAL(INTEGER n) RETURNS INTEGER

.   IF $n = 0$ THEN RETURN 1

.   ELSE   RETURN n * FACTORIAL($n-1$)

Andreas Sofroniou

The advantage of recursion is that it is often a simple restatement of a precise definition, one that avoids the bookkeeping details of an iterative solution.

At the machine-language level, loops and conditionals are implemented with branch instructions that say "jump to" a new point in the program.

The "goto" statement in higher-level languages expresses the same operation but is rarely used because it makes it difficult for humans to follow the "flow" of a program.

Some languages, such as Java and Ada, do not allow it.

Data structures

Whereas control structures organize algorithms, data structures organize information. In particular, data structures specify types of data, and thus which operations can be performed on them, while eliminating the need for a programmer to keep track of memory addresses. Simple data structures include integers, real numbers, Booleans (true/false), and characters or character strings. Compound data structures are formed by combining one or more data types.

The most important compound data structures are the array, a homogeneous collection of data, and the record, a heterogeneous collection. An array may represent a vector of numbers, a list of strings, or a collection of vectors (an array of arrays, or mathematical matrix). A record might store employee information—name, title, and salary. An array of records, such as a table of employees, is a collection of elements, each of which is heterogeneous. Conversely, a record might contain a vector— i.e., an array.

Record components, or fields, are selected by name; for example, E.SALARY might represent the salary field of record E. An array element is selected by its position or index; *A*[10] is the element at position 10 in array *A*. A FOR loop (definite iteration) can thus run through an array with index limits (FIRST TO LAST in the following example) in order to sum its elements:

- FOR *i* ← FIRST TO LAST

- SUM ← SUM + *A*[*i*]

Arrays and records have fixed sizes. Structures that can grow are built with dynamic allocation, which provides new storage as required. These data structures

Andreas Sofroniou

have components, each containing data and references to further components (in machine terms, their addresses).

Such self-referential structures have recursive definitions. A bin-tree (binary tree) for example, either is empty or contains a root component with data and left and right bin-tree "children."

Such bin-trees implement tables of information efficiently. Subroutines to operate on them are naturally recursive; the following routine prints out all the elements of a bin-tree (each is the root of some sub-tree):

- PROCEDURE TRAVERSE(ROOT: BINTREE)

- IF NOT(EMPTY(ROOT))

- TRAVERSE(ROOT.LEFT)

- PRINT ROOT.DATA

- TRAVERSE(ROOT.RIGHT)

- **ENDIF**

Abstract data types (ADTs) are important for large-scale programming. They package data structures and operations on them, hiding internal details.

For example, an ADT table provides insertion and lookup operations to users while keeping the underlying structure, whether an array, list, or binary tree, invisible.

In object-oriented languages, classes are ADTs and objects are instances of them.

The following object-oriented pseudocode example assumes that there is an ADT bin-tree and a "super-class" COMPARABLE, characterizing data for which there is a comparison operation (such as "<" for integers). It defines a new ADT, TABLE, that hides its data-representation and provides operations appropriate to tables.

This class is polymorphic—defined in terms of an element-type parameter of the COMPARABLE class. Any instance of it must specify that type, here a class with employee data (the COMPARABLE declaration means that PERS_REC must provide a comparison operation to sort records).

Implementation details are omitted.

- CLASS TABLE OF <COMPARABLE T>

  - PRIVATE DATA: BINTREE OF <T>

  - PUBLIC INSERT(ITEM: T)

  - PUBLIC   LOOKUP(ITEM: T) RETURNS BOOLEAN

  - END

- CLASS PERS_REC: COMPARABLE

  - PRIVATE NAME: STRING

- **PRIVATE POSITION: {STAFF, SUPERVISOR, MANAGER}**

- **PRIVATE SALARY: REAL**

- **PUBLIC COMPARE (R: PERS_REC) RETURNS BOOLEAN**

- **END**

- **EMPLOYEES: TABLE <PERS_REC>**

TABLE makes public only its own operations; thus, if it is modified to use an array or list rather than a bintree, programs that use it cannot detect the change.

This information hiding is essential to managing complexity in large programs.

It divides them into small parts, with "contracts" between the parts; here the TABLE class contracts to provide lookup and insertion operations, and its users contract to use only the operations so publicized.

COMPUTERS AND SYSTEMS ENGINEERING BACKGROUND

Systems engineering

Systems engineering profited from the advent of computers and the subsequent development of powerful, high-level programming languages, which affected the field in two principal ways.

First, they provided new tools for analyzing complex systems by means of extensive calculations or direct simulation.

In the second place, they could be used to digest large amounts of data or as actual constituents of complex systems, especially those concerned largely with information transmission.

Andreas Sofroniou

This opened up the possibility of processing information as well as simply transmitting it in such systems (see also information processing).

The impact of military weapons problems on systems engineering began soon after World War II. A landmark date was 1945, when the development of Nike Ajax, a U.S. air defence missile system, was initiated.

In 1945 available rocket propulsion seemed barely sufficient to give the missile a satisfactory tactical range. It was discovered that achievable range depended on several parameters, such as the weight and size of the warhead, fineness of the missile's aerodynamic design, degree of manoeuvrability provided by the control system, and shape of the trajectory and average speed along it.

Thus an effective systems engineering effort was mounted in which a variety of combinations of the missile's properties were explored, with the objective of achieving the best balance between range and other tactical characteristics.

Control and feedback questions were also important aspects of the overall systems problem. The whole system was in fact a gigantic feedback loop because the missile was controlled by orders sent it from a ground computer, and the computer input included information on what the tracking radar observed the missile to be doing.

Thus there was a closed feedback loop from missile to computer and back to the missile again.

There were also such subsidiary feedback loops as that of the autopilot controlling the attitude of the missile, and the dynamic response of the system was further affected by the need to process the radar signals to remove radar "jitter."

The analysis of such elaborate dynamical systems involving interlaced feedback paths has become an important special part of the general systems area.

In the 1950s and 1960s systems engineering also grew in other directions, largely as a result of weapons systems projects associated with the Cold War. Thus the Ajax study was concerned with the dynamics of a single isolated missile.

On the other hand, the defence systems that grew up in the 1950s involved the coordinated operation of a large number of missiles, guns, interceptors, and radar installations scattered over a considerable area.

These were all held together by a large digital computer, which thus became the central element of the system. The SAGE (semiautomatic ground environment) system in the United States is a good example.

During the same years the systems approach also became increasingly identified with management functions.

Thus the phrase "systems engineering and technical direction" came into use to describe the role of a systems engineer responsible for both the initial planning of a project and its subsequent management. So-called planning, programming, and budgeting (PPB) techniques were developed to provide similar combinations of systems engineering and financial management.

In non-military fields systems engineering has developed along similar though more modest lines.

Early applications were likely to stress feedback control systems in large-scale

Andreas Sofroniou

automated production facilities, such as steel-rolling mills and petroleum refineries.

Later applications stressed computer-based management information and control systems somewhat like those that had earlier been developed for air defence.

In more recent years the systems approach has occasionally been applied to much larger civilian enterprises, such as the planning of new cities.

SYSTEMS ANALYSIS HISTORY

Systems analysis

In information processing this is a phase of systems engineering. The principal objective of the systems-analysis phase is the specification of what the system needs to do to meet the requirements of end users. In the systems-design phase such specifications are converted to a hierarchy of charts that define the data required and the processes to be carried out on the data so that they can be expressed as instructions of a computer program.

Many information systems are implemented with generic software, rather than with such custom-built programs.

Andreas Sofroniou

Construction of system

The construction of a system is as complex as a house built in a swamp. It requires careful planning and design. Just as a house must have an architect's plan, so does a system. It must have requirements, system objectives, and a blueprint; the Diagrammatic Representation of Systems

In general, it must be well noticed that every system structured is an answer to the users' problems and requirements. The solutions will be based on the studies of the current systems (manual and computerised), and the problems and requirements catalogue.

The design of the system will be based on how the users work and what suits the overall business environment. Whilst analysing the users' needs, the system analyst will proceed with the logical stages, by listening, interviewing, and having walkthroughs and reviews with users and colleagues.

Prior to proceeding into the physical stages development, the system analysts, designers and managers involved, will seek approval from the appropriate groups of people. Within the physical stages and during the construction of the system, the system builders will test and make the necessary alterations to the modules being implemented.

The users' systems acceptance will include all the necessary documentation and all the training and support required to ensure that the new system or module is successful.

Background of structured analysis

The background of structured analysis and designing as an information engineering methodology, a technique-driven approach,

Andreas Sofroniou

started in 1972. Between 1980 and 1982, Gane and Sarson and Yourdon methodologies were extensively used. In 1983, business started using the information engineering automated version. By 1989, the information engineering development paths underwent further evolution. In 1992, the business re-engineering and object-oriented versions were introduced.

The need to control and manage the ever-increasing amounts of all organisational data being created, particularly computer-generated data, has gained recognition. However, because data management automates the processes used within a company, implementation is not easy. Several data management suppliers have begun requesting that a full systems and business analysis is undertaken prior to system implementation.

These show where existing processes need to be changed and determines exactly what the data management system needs to do within each unique organisation. It, therefore, provides the platform for successful systems architecture and management introduction and avoids the many pitfalls that so many companies have experienced in attempting to develop and install a new management system.

Rapid prototyping is gaining acceptance. Companies are using this method to obtain system design models in weeks rather than months, dramatically reducing lead-times and enabling better decisions and choice of system modules to be made.

A Systems Analyst in his/her approach defines the whole project, modularises it into manageable sections and proceeds in a logical manner according to the clear principles of user involvement.

The tasks are always broken down into structured, goal-oriented, meaningful units of work. The end result of these structured sets of tasks is applicable to the development path of:

- **Information Strategy Planning,**

- **Business Area Analysis,**

- **Business Design/Technical Design,**

- **Construction,**

- **Transition,**

- **Production.**

The above stages can be used by Analysts, Designers, Project Managers, Directors and Trainers in information technology methods to suit the technical and the user environment.

New techniques have been introduced that dramatically reduce the time taken to solve business and system problems. The result is that it is now possible to take the requirements, analyse, and view the results in days or weeks, rather than months. This, of course, makes analysis possible and cost-effective within the design process, rather than a special system task.

Recent years have seen further development in business and systems analysis software. Product releases of leading software houses have not only made systems architecture easier for everyday system engineers, but faster too. Closer links to CASE (Computer-aided Software Engineering) systems have made analysis simpler, while new interfaces make analysis understandable to users.

The term systems analysis is used in many computer installations in different ways. In fact, for most development projects it means the following:

Andreas Sofroniou

- **Fact finding,**

- **Operational analysis,**

- **Business system design.**

System analysis for an organisation means that the analyst has more detailed work to do by establishing with the users that there is a justification for developing a new system.

Systems engineering

Systems engineering is used for the design of complex systems with many interacting elements so as to optimize performance in some agreed way.

Systems engineering grew out of operational research, a discipline developed in the UK during World War II in an attempt to solve wartime logistical problems.

The invention of the digital computer was a key influence on the development of systems engineering as an interdisciplinary area, since rapidly evolving information technology not only increased the complexity of engineered systems many times, but also provided the tools with which to analyse, design, and control such complex systems.

Application areas of systems engineering vary widely, including the core technological fields of automation, control systems, and mechatronics, but also public services, large commercial organizations, and ecological management and conservation.

In systems engineering, the problem to be solved is first formulated in as precise a manner as possible by specifying system goals, performance measures, and important variables.

Next, the problem is broken down, the important sub-systems and their interrelationships (interfaces) being identified. The individual sub-systems are then modelled and designed, followed by design of the complete system.

Finally, the sub-systems and then the complete system are implemented and tested. Each individual stage may itself involve the repeated validation, testing, and possible modification of the various earlier stages.

Provided the problem has been appropriately identified, specified, and partitioned, the modelling and design of individual system elements will often be carried out by specialist engineers, together with experts in reliability and risk assessment, mathematical modelling, computer simulation, and so on.

An important task of the systems engineer as 'technical generalist' is to ensure that the

Andreas Sofroniou

eventual integration of the work of such specialist individuals or teams results in an overall system conforming to specification.

Systems analysis

Systems analysis is a stage of a system's development which includes the investigation, analysis, design, implementation, and evaluation of an information system, usually with the aim of computerizing some human activity.

The main functions of systems analysis may be broken down as follows.

First, the problem to be solved (for example, the computerization of a business's accounting system) must be accurately defined.

The existing system is then investigated to understand how it works, using techniques such as flow charting and decision tables (tables that indicate actions to be taken under various conditions, the decision being the selection between alternatives).

Next, the results of the investigation are analysed and used as the basis for the design of a new system, making optimum use of the available computer hardware, software, and staffing resources.

The new system is then implemented and evaluated, and those people concerned with using and running it are taught how to operate and maintain it efficiently.

Flow chart

Flow charting is a design technique depicting the order of logical steps (algorithm) required to solve a problem prior to writing a computer software program, or designing computer system using systems analysis techniques.

Flow charts use specific symbols to represent particular operations, so that the logic of the chart is immediately apparent. Each symbol is equivalent to a statement or group of statements in the program, which facilitates the eventual writing and testing of the program, and the correction of errors. However, with the advent of software engineering, flow charting is in decline.

Menu (in computing)

This is a list of program or function options which is presented to the user by a computer on a visual display unit. The user selects the desired option by keyboard or mouse. Menu-based software is used extensively in interactive systems because of its convenience and ease of use.

133

Interactive system

This is a computer system which responds to instructions from the user as they are given. The system responds fast enough to allow transactions to be completed almost continuously. The success or failure of each transaction is immediately obvious from the way in which the computer responds. The instructions are input via a device such as a mouse or keyboard.

Cybernetics

Cybernetics (from the Greek, *kubernetes*, steersman) is the study of communication and control systems in machines, animals, and organizations.

The discipline developed immediately after World War II, when control-systems and systems-engineering techniques were applied successfully to certain neurological problems.

The term cybernetics was first applied in English by Wiener. Cybernetics is characterized by a concentration on the flow of information (rather than energy or material) within a system, and on the use of feedback or 'goal-directed activity' in both technological artefacts and living organisms. Major areas of cybernetic study have been biological control systems, automation, animal communication, and artificial intelligence (AI).

The recent rapid expansion of AI as a subject area, together with the development of knowledge-based systems and neural networks, have renewed interest in the general cybernetic approach, although the term 'cybernetics' itself is now rarely used.

SECURITY AND SYSTEM ASSURANCE

Systems security

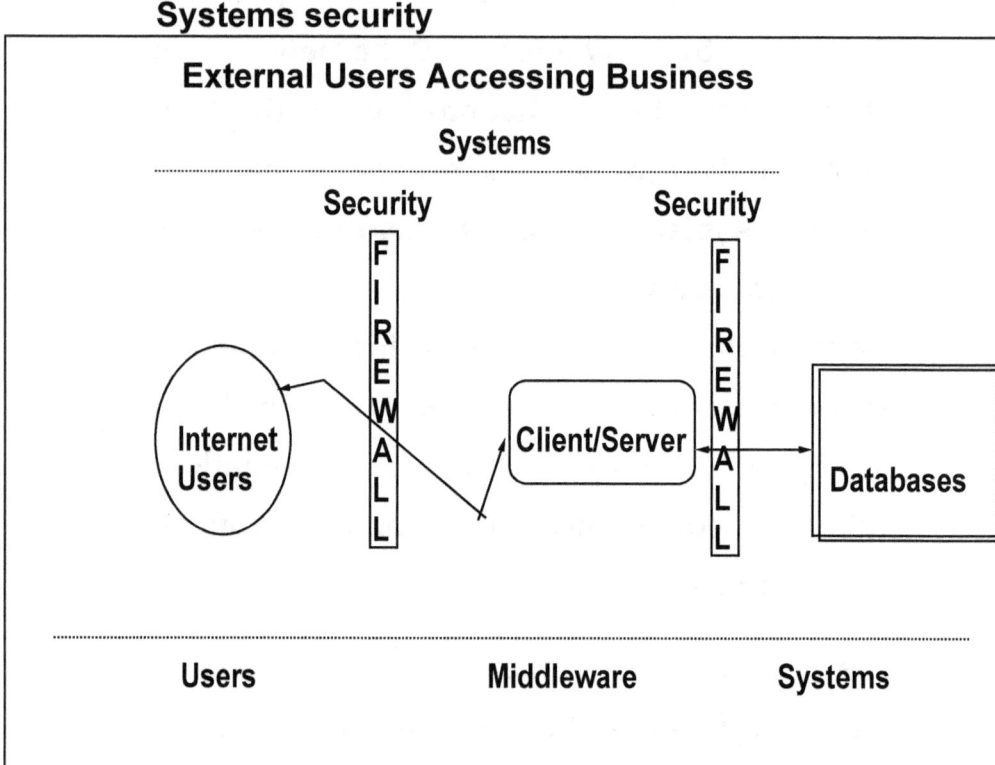

Computer security has become a challenge dominated by the improvements to information technology.

Techniques are being developed to make access to systems harder. In recent years, much work has been done to make the computer recognise individual characteristics, unique to the user, such as eye contact, a signature, fingerprinting, or even the genetic print of DNA.

With users and companies becoming more dependent upon computer systems, the privacy and reliability of such systems are becoming critical aspects of design.

Systems Assurance, a term which is currently popular, of a system embraces the parts of systems design which reduce the risk of both the fraudulent use of the system and lengthy recovery times in the event of a system's failure.

In many companies, one of the few problems that have to be resolved quickly is:

- Privacy,

- Fraudulent entry of data,

- Policing, a system must do more than just reporting violation,

- Effective restricted access at varying levels to different users,

- Recording access violations.

Users and companies are becoming more and more dependent upon resilience of computer-based systems.

Computer systems can fail for a number of reasons.

Failures due to:

- Telecommunications,

- Hardware,

- Software,

- Networking.

Whichever the cause of the failure, the user will expect that the system can be recovered quickly and that the applications are free from data corruption.

Inconsistencies within applications can result in:

- Users losing confidence in the system,

- Lengthy investigation into the cause of failure,

- Protected systems down time whilst the data sets are reconstructed from source documentation.

Therefore, one significant aspect of recovery is the time taken to reconstruct application data sets.

The most straightforward method of recovering is to duplicate them by backup. The advantage of a backup is that recovery after failure is extremely fast.

Andreas Sofroniou

In various sensitive applications, frequent auditing is recommended. As a minimum, a daily control report should be produced, reconciling balances on the opening and closing versions of data sets.

This report should also show in detail the origins of all transactions processed during the reporting period.

With the number of computer applications continuing to grow and with a similar increase in the number of people using them, a new type of back-up service is needed.

To meet the demand, a number of companies have introduced guides to their applications, which include various types of catalogues. The catalogue, in fact, serves as a comprehensive system engineering tool.

Details on system applications, specifications, and service requirements are made available to all users. If a user is not sure what documents are needed, he/she can start by looking at the full index.

Companies are even making available dedicated internal e-mail messages and Internet pages, the latter being interactive and intelligent. Newsletters are published, which keep the users informed of new product developments, interesting applications, and other IT activities.

The widespread use of computers throughout business and the rapid growth of Internet connectivity mean that computer security should concern all organisations.

One simple measure to prevent unauthorised outsiders dialling into the system is to install dial-back modems.

However, this security measure is easy to side-step. Likewise, calling-line identification, which permits the computer to identify the calling number and refuse access if it is not recognised, can be bypassed by the experienced people.

Encryption is essential for the transmission of any material passing down the line, broadband, and wi-fi.

A simple method is to employ software which uses the same code at either end to encode and decode data.

The next level is to impose a code of the day, using an encryption device card which is synchronised with a similar calculator card within the network.

The most complex form of encryption available is the digital signature. Each user has a private key linked to a public key made available on an electronic notice board.

The user encodes the message with the private key and the message can be decoded by anyone holding the allocated public key.

However, any message encoded with the public key can be decoded only by the holder of the private key.

SOFTWARE CONSIDERATIONS

Software requirements

Developing large systems require a range of software to achieve the overall objective. Depending upon the application and hardware types, this range of software at best could be totally packaged, or at worst may need to be completely written specially for the system. Software in a project is like a jigsaw puzzle.

Each piece fulfils a role and each piece must integrate with other pieces to make the complete system.

The basic types of software used are:

- Applications software,

- Conversational software,

- Database management software,

- System development software,

Andreas Sofroniou

- Network software,

- System support software.

Applying hardware and software knowledge to system designing and the development of systems enables System Architects to choose individual applications from a range of developers and bring these together into a single system that best meets the needs of the company and its tasks, transparently, sharing data.

It also enables standard software, such as spreadsheets, word-processing, presentation packages, and databases, to be linked to engineering software.

The flexibility this gives is far better for users than the traditional closed systems environment that forms the basis of many computing software packages. However, to take advantage of this environment the system developers must totally restructure their approach to system building, a complex, and daunting task.

144

STRUCTURED SYSTEMS ANALYSIS

Structured methodology

As a background to structured methodology, it is worth mentioning that it all started with IBM and the problems this giant of computing was facing with the programming problems. IBM called in psychologist Larry Constantine who, as the story goes, diagnosed that the programmers were projecting their own individual perceptions of how the specifications were written.

Larry Constantine's write-up on a structured method included ideas from his psycho-physiological studies and terms such as afferent and efferent. His suggestions worked for IBM and soon after, others followed with variations. Names such as Gane and Sarson, Yourdon, James Martin, and other gurus, who again were followed by BIS Modus, LBMS-

Andreas Sofroniou

LSDM and with CCTA-SSADM and many, many more familiar names.

The differences among the protagonists were not of any consequence. Gane and Sarson used to say that all details could be gathered within a diagram and then modularise into smaller sections within boundaries. Yourdon maintained that anything bigger than an A4 paper was too complicated. Now-a-days, everybody is recommending five boxes on an average within a boundary, maximum seven and three the minimum. Any more than seven boxes and the analyst will take into consideration the possibility of decomposing to a lower level.

The point is that, instead of just picking up the keyboard of the dummy terminal and starting to program, everybody in the commercial world is now following a structured method. Whether the systems designed are successful or not, depends on the training and experience the systems engineers bear with them. In a similar way this is what the contents of this book are trying to assimilate.

Requirements for analysis

Systems Analysis consists of an evolving set of tools and techniques which have grown out of the success of structured designing. The underlying concept is the building of a logical model, a non-physical system, using a diagrammatic representation which enables the users and analysts to get a clear and common understanding of the required system. How its parts fit together and how it answers to the users' needs.

Since Computer-aided Software Engineering (CASE) tools are used to build a logical model, structured methodology involves building a system by successive refinement by:

- Producing an overall system dataflow diagram (DFD),

- Developing detailed dataflows,

- Defining the detail of data structure and process logic,

The whole of the analysis and designing of the system is done by employing a top-down method for:

- Analysing,

- Designing,

- Developing,

- Testing.

It is recognised that good development involves iteration, and an Analyst has to be prepared to refine the logical model and the physical design in the light of information resulting from the use of an early version of that model, or design. This may involve some reverse engineering of the processes of an earlier physical system, or an earlier version of the analysis exercise.

In many ways, systems analysis and designing is the toughest part of the development of an information technology system.

The problems encountered by an Analyst in a company environment will include:

- Technical difficulty of the work,

- Demand of knowledge of current technology,

- Political difficulties that arise,

- Several conflicting interest user groups,

- Communication difficulties among people of different backgrounds,

Andreas Sofroniou

- Different views, requirements and priorities.

It is the compounding of these difficulties that makes systems analysis so demanding. It is a fact that the analyst becomes the middleman between user groups and has the intuitive approach for the users' problems and their solutions. The analyst must bring forward what is currently possible in an onrushing technology and what is optimum for the business run by people - making the match in a way which is acceptable to all.

Even with the best CASE tool, no methodology will enable the analyst to know what is in a user's mind and has no way of showing a tangible model of the system, apart from the diagrams of the logical phases and their short descriptions.

On the other hand, it is hard for the users to imagine what the new system is going to do for them, until it is actually up and running, by which time it may be too late to perform any costly post-implementation repairs and additions.

To begin with, in order to ease the communication with the users, an analyst can use the tools of structured systems analysis to prepare a functional specification which:

- Is comprehended and agreed by the users,

- Sets out the logical requirements of the system without dictating a physical implementation,

- Expresses preferences and trade-offs.

The building of a logical model which clearly communicates to users what the systems will and will not do is crucially important.

The users cannot afford to wait until the system is operational, before they see what they get. The analysing and designing of the logical phases are, therefore, of paramount importance in telling the users what to expect.

Andreas Sofroniou

SYSTEMS PROGRAMMING

Computer software

These is used for the development of computer software that is part of a computer operating system or other control program, especially as used in computer networks.

Systems programming covers data and program management, including operating systems, control programs, network software, and database management systems.

Software

Software is the instructions that tell a computer what to do. Software comprises the entire set of programs, procedures, and routines associated with the operation of a computer system.

The term was coined to differentiate these instructions from hardware—*i.e.,* the physical components of a computer system. A set of instructions that directs a computer's hardware to perform a task is called a program, or software program.

The two main types of software are system software and application software. System software controls a computer's internal functioning, chiefly through an operating system (*q.v.*), and also controls such peripherals as monitors, printers, and storage devices.

Application software, by contrast, directs the computer to execute commands given by the user and may be said to include any program that processes data for a user.

Application software thus includes word processors, spreadsheets, database management, inventory and payroll programs, and many other "applications." A third software category is that of network software, which coordinates communication between the computers linked in a network.

Software is typically stored on an external long-term memory device, such as a hard drive or magnetic diskette. When the program is in use, the computer reads it from the storage device and temporarily places the instructions in random access memory (RAM).

The process of storing and then performing the instructions is called "running," or "executing," a program.

By contrast, software programs and procedures that are permanently stored in a computer's memory using a read-only (ROM) technology are called firmware, or "hard software."

Operating system

This is the program that manages a computer's resources, especially the allocation of those resources among other programs. Typical resources include the central processing unit (CPU), computer memory, file storage, input/output (I/O) devices, and network connections.

Management tasks include scheduling resource use to avoid conflicts and interference between programs. Unlike most programs, which complete a task and terminate, an operating system runs indefinitely and terminates only when the computer is turned off.

Modern multiprocessing operating systems allow many processes to be active, where each process is a "thread" of computation being used to execute a program. One form of multiprocessing is called time-sharing, which lets many users share computer access by rapidly switching between them.

Time-sharing must guard against interference between users' programs, and most systems use virtual memory, in which the memory, or "address space," used by a program may reside in secondary memory (such as on a magnetic hard disk drive) when not in immediate use, to be swapped back to occupy the faster main computer memory on demand.

This virtual memory both increases the address space available to a program and helps to prevent programs from interfering with each other, but it requires careful control by the operating system and a set of allocation tables to keep track of memory use.

Perhaps the most delicate and critical task for a modern operating system is allocation of the CPU; each process is allowed to use the CPU for a limited time, which may be a

Andreas Sofroniou

fraction of a second, and then must give up control and become suspended until its next turn. Switching between processes must itself use the CPU while protecting all data of the processes.

The first digital computers had no operating systems. They ran one program at a time, which had command of all system resources, and a human operator would provide any special resources needed. The first operating systems were developed in the mid-1950s.

These were small "supervisor programs" that provided basic I/O operations (such as controlling punch card readers and printers) and kept accounts of CPU usage for billing. Supervisor programs also provided multiprogramming capabilities to enable several programs to run at once.

This was particularly important so that these early multimillion-dollar machines would not be idle during slow I/O operations.

Computers acquired more powerful operating systems in the 1960s with the emergence of time-sharing, which required a system to manage multiple users sharing CPU time and terminals.

Two early time-sharing systems were CTSS (Compatible Time Sharing System), developed at the Massachusetts Institute of Technology, and the Dartmouth College Basic System, developed at Dartmouth College.

Other multi-programmed systems included Atlas, at the University of Manchester, England, and IBM's OS/360, probably the most complex software package of the 1960s.

After 1972 the Multics system for General Electric Co.'s GE 645 computer (and later for Honeywell Inc.'s computers) became the most

Andreas Sofroniou

sophisticated system, with most of the multiprogramming and time-sharing capabilities that later became standard.

The minicomputers of the 1970s had limited memory and required smaller operating systems.

The most important operating system of that period was UNIX, developed by AT&T for large minicomputers as a simpler alternative to Multics.

It became widely used in the 1980s, in part because it was free to universities and in part because it was designed with a set of tools that were powerful in the hands of skilled programmers.

More recently, Linux, an open-source version of UNIX developed in part by a group led by Finnish computer science student Linus Torvalds and in part by a group led by American computer programmer Richard

Andreas Sofroniou

Stallman, has become popular on personal computers as well as on larger "mainframe" computers.

In addition to such general-purpose systems, special-purpose operating systems run on small computers that control assembly lines, aircraft, and even home appliances.

They are real-time systems, designed to provide rapid response to sensors and to use their inputs to control machinery.

From the standpoint of a user or an application program, an operating system provides services.

Some of these are simple user commands like "dir"—show the files on a disk—while others are low-level "system calls" that a graphics program might use to display an image.

In either case the operating system provides appropriate access to its objects, the tables of disk locations in one case and the routines to transfer data to the screen in the other. Some of its routines, those that manage the CPU and memory, are generally accessible only to other portions of the operating system.

Contemporary operating systems for personal computers commonly provide a graphical user interface (GUI).

The GUI may be an intrinsic part of the system, as in the older Apple Inc.'s Mac OS and Microsoft Corporation's Windows OS; in others it is a set of programs that depend on an underlying system, as in the X Window system for UNIX and Apple's Mac OS X.

Operating systems also provide network services and file-sharing capabilities—even the ability to share resources between systems of different types, such as Windows and UNIX.

Such sharing has become feasible through the introduction of network protocols (communication rules) such as the Internet's TCP/IP.

Computer network

This is where two or more computers that are connected with one another for the purpose of communicating data electronically.

Besides physically connecting computer and communication devices, a network system serves the important function of establishing a cohesive architecture that allows a variety of equipment types to transfer information in a near-seamless fashion.

Two popular architectures are ISO Open Systems Interconnection (OSI) and IBM's Systems Network Architecture (SNA).

Two basic network types are local-area networks (LANs) and wide-area (or long-haul) networks. LANs connect computers and peripheral devices in a limited physical area, such as a business office, laboratory, or college campus, by means of permanent links (wires, cables, fibre optics) that transmit data rapidly.

A typical LAN consists of two or more personal computers, printers, and high-capacity disk-storage devices called file servers, which enable each computer on the network to access a common set of files.

LAN operating system software, which interprets input and instructs networked devices,

- Allows users to communicate with each other;

- Share the printers and storage equipment;

Andreas Sofroniou

- Simultaneously access centrally located processors, data, or programs (instruction sets).

LAN users may also access other LANs or tap into wide-area networks. LANs with similar architectures are linked by "bridges," which act as transfer points. LANs with different architectures are linked by "gateways," which convert data as it passes between systems.

Wide-area networks connect computers and smaller networks to larger networks over greater geographic areas, including different continents.

They may link the computers by means of cables, optical fibres, or satellites, but their users commonly access the networks via a modem (a device that allows computers to communicate over telephone lines).

The largest wide-area network is the Internet, a collection of networks and gateways linking

Andreas Sofroniou

millions of computer users on every continent.

Database management system (DBMS)

This is the system used for quick search and retrieval of information from a database. The DBMS determines how data are stored and retrieved. It must address problems such as security, accuracy, consistency among different records, response time, and memory requirements.

These issues are most significant for database systems on computer networks. Ever-higher processing speeds are required for efficient database management. Relational DBMSs, in which data are organized into a series of tables ("relations") that are easily reorganized for accessing data in different ways, are the most widely used today.

Andreas Sofroniou

INFORMATION PROCESSING

Information dissemination

This is the processing for the acquisition, recording, organization, retrieval, display, and dissemination of information.

In recent years, the term has often been applied to computer-based operations specifically.

In popular usage, the term *information* refers to facts and opinions provided and received during the course of daily life: one obtains information directly from other living beings, from mass media, from electronic data banks, and from all sorts of observable phenomena in the surrounding environment.

A person using such facts and opinions generates more information, some of which is communicated to others during discourse, by instructions, in letters and documents, and through other media.

Information organized according to some logical relationships is referred to as a body of knowledge, to be acquired by systematic exposure or study.

Application of knowledge (or skills) yields expertise, and additional analytic or experiential insights are said to constitute instances of wisdom.

Use of the term *information* is not restricted exclusively to its communication via natural language.

Information is also registered and communicated through art and by facial expressions and gestures or by such other physical responses as shivering.

Moreover, every living entity is endowed with information in the form of a genetic code.

These information phenomena permeate the physical and mental world, and their variety is such that it has defied so far all attempts at a unified definition of information.

Interest in information phenomena increased dramatically in the 20th century, and today they are the objects of study in a number of disciplines, including philosophy, physics, biology, linguistics, information and computer science, electronic and communications engineering, management science, and the social sciences.

On the commercial side, the information service industry has become one of the newer industries worldwide.

Almost all other industries—manufacturing and service—are increasingly concerned with information and its handling.

The different, though often overlapping, viewpoints and phenomena of these fields

Andreas Sofroniou

lead to different (and sometimes conflicting) concepts and "definitions" of information.

This article touches on such concepts as they relate to information processing. In treating the basic elements of information processing, it distinguishes between information in analogue and digital form, and it describes its acquisition, recording, organization, retrieval, display, and techniques of dissemination.

A separate article, information system, covers methods for organizational control and dissemination of information.

Andreas Sofroniou

GENERAL CONSIDERATIONS

Basic concepts

Interest in how information is communicated and how its carriers convey meaning has occupied, since the time of pre-Socratic philosophers, the field of inquiry called semiotics, the study of signs and sign phenomena. Signs are the irreducible elements of communication and the carriers of meaning.

The American philosopher, mathematician, and physicist Charles S. Peirce is credited with having pointed out the three dimensions of signs, which are concerned with, respectively, the body or medium of the sign, the object that the sign designates, and the interpretant or interpretation of the sign.

Andreas Sofroniou

Peirce recognized that the fundamental relations of information are essentially triadic; in contrast, all relations of the physical sciences are reducible to dyadic (binary) relations.

Another American philosopher, Charles W. Morris, designated these three sign dimensions syntactic, semantic, and pragmatic, the names by which they are known today.

Information processes are executed by information processors. For a given information processor, whether physical or biological, a token is an object, devoid of meaning, that the processor recognizes as being totally different from other tokens.

A group of such unique tokens recognized by a processor constitutes its basic "alphabet"; for example, the dot, dash, and space constitute the basic token alphabet of a

Andreas Sofroniou

Morse-code processor. Objects that carry meaning are represented by patterns of tokens called symbols.

The latter combine to form symbolic expressions that constitute inputs to or outputs from information processes, and are stored in the processor memory.

Information processors

Information processors are components of an information system, which is a class of constructs. An abstract model of an information system features four basic elements: processor, memory, receptor, and effector.

The processor has several functions:

(1) To carry out elementary information processes on symbolic expressions,

Andreas Sofroniou

(2) To store temporarily in the processor's short-term memory the input and output expressions on which these processes operate and that they generate,

(3) To schedule execution of these processes, and

(4) To change this sequence of operations in accordance with the contents of the short-term memory.

The memory stores symbolic expressions, including those that represent composite information processes, called programs. The two other components, the receptor and the effector, are input and output mechanisms whose functions are, respectively, to receive symbolic expressions or stimuli from the external environment for manipulation by the processor and to emit the processed structures back to the environment.

Andreas Sofroniou

The power of this abstract model of an information-processing system is provided by the ability of its component processors to carry out a small number of elementary information processes: reading; comparing; creating, modifying, and naming; copying; storing; and writing.

The model, which is representative of a broad variety of such systems, has been found useful to explicate man-made information systems implemented on sequential information processors.

Because it has been recognized that in nature information processes are not strictly sequential, increasing attention has been focused since 1980 on the study of the human brain as an information processor of the parallel type.

The cognitive sciences, the interdisciplinary field that focuses on the study of the human mind, have contributed to the development of neuro-computers, a new class of parallel, distributed-information processors that mimic the functioning of the human brain, including its capabilities for self-organization and learning.

So-called neural networks, which are mathematical models inspired by the neural circuit network of the human brain, are increasingly finding applications in areas such as pattern recognition, control of industrial processes, and finance, as well as in many research disciplines.

Resource and commodity information

In the late 20th century, information acquired two major utilitarian connotations. On the one hand, it is considered an economic resource, somewhat on par with other resources such as labour, material, and capital.

This view stems from evidence that the possession, manipulation, and use of information can increase the cost-effectiveness of many physical and cognitive processes.

The rise in information-processing activities in industrial manufacturing as well as in human problem solving has been remarkable.

Analysis of one of the three traditional divisions of the economy, the service sector, shows a sharp increase in information-intensive activities since the beginning of the 20th century. By 1975 these activities accounted for half of the labour force of the United States, giving rise to the so-called information society.

As an individual and societal resource, information has some interesting characteristics that separate it from the traditional notions of economic resources.

Unlike other resources, information is expansive, with limits apparently imposed only by time and human cognitive capabilities.

Its expansiveness is attributable to the following:

(1) It is naturally diffusive,

(2) It reproduces rather than being consumed through use, and

(3) It can be shared only, not exchanged in transactions.

At the same time, information is compressible, both syntactically and semantically.

Coupled with its ability to be substituted for other economic resources, its transportability at very high speeds, and its ability to impart advantages to the holder of information, these characteristics are at the base of such

Andreas Sofroniou

societal industries as research, education, publishing, marketing, and even politics.

Societal concern with the husbanding of information resources has extended from the traditional domain of libraries and archives to encompass organizational, institutional, and governmental information under the umbrella of information resource management.

The second perception of information is that it is an economic commodity, which helps to stimulate the worldwide growth of a new segment of national economies—the information service sector.

Taking advantage of the properties of information and building on the perception of its individual and societal utility and value, this sector provides a broad range of information products and services. By 1992 the market share of the U.S. information service sector had grown to about $25 billion.

178

This was equivalent to about one-seventh of the country's computer market, which, in turn, represented roughly 40 percent of the global market in computers in that year.

However, the probable convergence of computers and television (which constitutes a market share 100 times larger than computers) and its impact on information services, entertainment, and education are likely to restructure the respective market shares of the information industry.

Elements of information processing

Humans receive information with their senses: sounds through hearing; images and text through sight; shape, temperature, and affection through touch; and odours through smell.

To interpret the signals received from the senses, humans have developed and learned

Andreas Sofroniou

complex systems of languages consisting of "alphabets" of symbols and stimuli and the associated rules of usage.

This has enabled them to recognize the objects they see, understand the messages they read or hear, and comprehend the signs received through the tactile and olfactory senses.

The carriers of information-conveying signs received by the senses are energy phenomena—audio waves, light waves, and chemical and electrochemical stimuli. In engineering parlance, humans are receptors of analogue signals; and, by a somewhat loose convention, the messages conveyed via these carriers are called analogue-form information, or simply analogue information.

Until the development of the digital computer, cognitive information was stored and processed only in analogue form, basically through the technologies of printing, photography, and telephony.

Although humans are adept at processing information stored in their memories, analogue information stored external to the mind is not processed easily.

Modern information technology greatly facilitates the manipulation of externally stored information as a result of its representation as digital signals—i.e., as the presence or absence of energy (electricity, light, or magnetism).

Information represented digitally in two-state, or binary, form is often referred to as digital information. Modern information systems are characterized by extensive metamorphoses of analogue and digital information. With respect to information storage and communication, the transition from analogue to digital information is so pervasive as to bring a historic transformation of the manner in which humans create, access, and use information.

Acquisition and recording of information in analogue form

The principal categories of information sources useful in modern information systems are text, video, and voice.

One of the first ways in which prehistoric humans communicated was by sound; sounds represented concepts such as pleasure, anger, and fear, as well as objects of the surrounding environment, including food and tools.

Sounds assumed their meaning by convention—namely, by the use to which they were consistently put. Combining parts of sound allowed representation of more complex concepts and gradually led to the development of speech and eventually to spoken "natural" languages.

For information to be communicated broadly, it needs to be stored external to human memory; because accumulation of human experience, knowledge, and learning would be severely limited without such storage, the development of writing systems was made necessary.

Civilization can be traced to the time when humans began to associate abstract shapes with concepts and with the sounds of speech that represented them. Early recorded representations were those of visually perceived objects and events, as, for example, the animals and activities depicted in Palaeolithic cave drawings.

The evolution of writing systems proceeded through the early development of

Andreas Sofroniou

pictographic languages, in which a symbol would represent an entire concept.

Such symbols would go through many metamorphoses of shape in which the resemblance between each symbol and the object it stood for gradually disappeared, but its semantic meaning would become more precise.

As the conceptual world of humans became larger, the symbols, called ideographs, grew in number.

Modern Chinese, a present-day result of this evolutionary direction of a pictographic writing system, has upwards of 50,000 ideographs.

At some point in the evolution of written languages, the method of representation shifted from the pictographic to the phonetic: speech sounds began to be represented by an alphabet of graphic symbols.

Combinations of a relatively small set of such symbols could stand for more complex concepts as words, phrases, and sentences.

The invention of the written phonetic alphabet is thought to have taken place during the 2nd millennium BC. The pragmatic advantages of alphabetic writing systems over the pictographic became apparent twice in the past millennium: after the invention of the movable-type printing press in the 15th century and again with the development of information processing by electronic means since the mid-1940s.

From the time early humans learned to represent concepts symbolically, they used whatever materials were readily available in nature for recording. The Sumerian cuneiform, a wedge-shaped writing system, was impressed by a stylus into soft clay tablets, which were subsequently hardened by drying in the sun or the oven.

The earliest Chinese writing, dating to the 2nd millennium BC, is preserved on animal bone and shell, while early writing in India was done on palm leaves and birch bark.

Applications of technology yielded other materials for writing. The Chinese had recorded their pictographs on silk, using brushes made from animal hair, long before they invented paper.

The Egyptians first wrote on cotton, but they began using papyrus sheets and rolls made from the fibrous lining of the papyrus plant during the 4th millennium BC. The reed brush and a palette of ink were the implements with which they wrote hieroglyphic script.

Writing on parchment, a material that was superior to papyrus and was made from the prepared skins of animals, became commonplace about 200 BC, some 300 years after its first recorded use, and the quill pen

Andreas Sofroniou

replaced the reed brush. By the 4th century AD, parchment came to be the principal writing material in Europe.

Paper was invented in China at the beginning of the 2nd century AD, and for some 600 years its use was confined to East Asia. In AD 751 Arab and Chinese armies clashed at the Battle of Talas, near Samarkand; among the Chinese taken captive were some papermakers from whom the Arabs learned the techniques.

From the 7th century on, paper became the dominant writing material of the Islamic world. Papermaking finally reached Spain and Sicily in the 12th century, and it took another three centuries before it was practiced in Germany.

With the invention of printing from movable type, typesetting became the standard method of creating copy.

Typesetting was an entirely manual operation until the adoption of a typewriter-like keyboard in the 19th century. In fact, it was the typewriter that mechanized the process of recording original text.

Although the typewriter was invented during the early 18th century in England, the first practical version, constructed by the American inventor Christopher Latham Sholes, did not appear until 1867. The mechanical typewriter finally found wide use after World War I. Today its electronic variant, the computer video terminal, is used pervasively to record original text.

Recording of original non-textual (image) information was a manual process until the development of photography during the early decades of the 19th century; drawing and carving were the principal early means of recording graphics. Other techniques were developed alongside printing—for example, etching in stone and metal.

The invention of film and the photographic process added a new dimension to information acquisition: for the first time, complex visual images of the real world could be captured accurately.

Photography provided a method of storing information in less space and more accurately than was previously possible with narrative information.

During the 20th century, versatile electromagnetic media opened up new possibilities for capturing original analogue information.

Magnetic audio tape is used to capture speech and music, and magnetic videotape provides a low-cost medium for recording analogue voice and video signals directly and simultaneously. Magnetic technology has other uses in the direct recording of analogue information, including alpha-numerics.

Magnetic characters, bar codes, and special marks are printed on checks, labels, and forms for subsequent sensing by magnetic or optical readers and conversion to digital form. Banks, educational institutions, and the retail industry rely heavily on this technology.

Nonetheless, paper and film continue to be the dominant media for direct storage of textual and visual information in analogue form.

Acquisition and recording of information in digital form

The versatility of modern information systems stems from their ability to represent information electronically as digital signals and to manipulate it automatically at exceedingly high speeds. Information is stored in binary devices, which are the basic components of digital technology.

Because these devices exist only in one of two states, information is represented in them either as the absence or the presence of energy (electric pulse). The two states of binary devices are conveniently designated by the binary digits, or bits, zero (0) and one (1).

In this manner, alphabetic symbols of natural-language writing systems can be represented digitally as combinations of zeros (no pulse) and ones (pulse). Tables of equivalences of alphanumeric characters and strings of binary digits are called coding systems, the counterpart of writing systems.

A combination of three binary digits can represent up to eight such characters; one comprising four digits, up to 16 characters; and so on.

The choice of a particular coding system depends on the size of the character set to be represented. The widely used systems are the American Standard Code for Information Interchange (ASCII), a seven- or eight-bit code representing the English alphabet, numerals, and certain special characters of the standard computer keyboard; and the corresponding eight-bit Extended Binary Coded Decimal Interchange Code (EBCDIC), used for computers produced by IBM (International Business Machines Corp.) and most compatible systems. The digital representation of a character by eight bits is called a byte.

The seven-bit ASCII code is capable of representing up to 128 alphanumeric and special characters—sufficient to accommodate the writing systems of many phonetic scripts, including Latin and Cyrillic.

Some alphabetic scripts require more than seven bits; for example, the Arabic alphabet, also used in the Urdu and Persian languages, has 28 consonantal characters (as well as a number of vowels and diacritical marks), but each of these may have four shapes, depending on its position in the word.

For digital representation of non-alphabetic writing systems, even the eight-bit code accommodating 256 characters is inadequate. Some writing systems that use Chinese characters, for example, have more than 50,000 ideographs (the minimal standard font for the Hanzi system in Chinese and the kanji system in Japanese has about 7,000 ideographs).

Digital representation of such scripts can be accomplished in three ways:

- One approach is to develop a phonetic character set; the Chinese Pinyin, the

Korean Hangul, and the Japanese hiragana phonetic schemes all have alphabetic sets similar in number to the Latin alphabet. As the use of phonetic alphabets in Oriental cultures is not yet widespread, they may be converted to ideographic by means of a dictionary lookup.

- A second technique is to decompose ideographs into a small number of elementary signs called strokes, the sum of which constitutes a shape-oriented, non-phonetic alphabet.

- The third approach is to use more than eight bits to encode the large numbers of ideographs; for instance, two bytes can represent uniquely more than 65,000 ideographs.

Because the eight-bit ASCII code is inadequate for a number of writing systems, either because they are non-alphabetic or because their phonetic scripts possess large numbers of diacritical marks, the computer industry in 1991 began formulating a new international coding standard based on 16 bits.

Recording media

Punched cards and perforated paper tape were once widely used to store data in binary form. Today they have been supplanted by media based on electromagnetic and electro-optic technologies except in a few special applications

Present-day storage media are of two types: random- and serial-, or sequential-, access. In random-access media (such as primary memory), the time required for accessing a given piece of data is independent of its location, while in serial-access media the

195

access time depends on the data's location and the position of the read-write head.

The typical serial-access medium is magnetic tape. The storage density of magnetic tape has increased considerably over the years, mainly by increases in the number of tracks packed across the width of the tape.

While magnetic tape remains a popular choice in applications requiring low-cost auxiliary storage and data exchange, new tape variants began entering the market of the 1990s.

Video recording tape has been adapted for digital storage, and digital audio tape (DAT) surpasses all tape storage devices in offering the highest areal data densities. DAT technology uses a helical-scan recording method in which both the tape and the recording head move simultaneously, which allows extremely high recording densities.

Early four-millimetre DAT cassettes had a capacity of up to eight billion bytes (eight gigabytes).

Another type of magnetic storage medium, the magnetic disk, provides rapid, random access to data. This device, developed in 1962, consists of either aluminium or a plastic platen coated with a metallic material.

Information is recorded on a disk by turning the charge of the read-write head on and off, which produces magnetic "dots" representing binary digits in circular tracks.

A block of data on a given track can be accessed without having to pass over a large portion of its contents sequentially, as in the case of tape. Data-retrieval time is thus reduced dramatically. Hard disk drives built into personal computers and workstations have storage capacities of up to several gigabytes. Large computers using disk cartridges can provide virtually unlimited mass storage.

During the 1970s the floppy disk—a small, flexible disk—was introduced for use in personal computers and other microcomputer systems. Compared with the storage capacity of the conventional hard disk, that of such a "soft" diskette is low—under three million characters. This medium is used primarily for loading and backing up personal computers.

An entirely different kind of recording and storage medium, the optical disc, became available during the early 1980s.

The optical disc makes use of laser technology: digital data are recorded by burning a series of microscopic holes, or pits, with a laser beam into thin metallic film on the surface of a $4^3/_4$-inch (12-centimetre) plastic disc. In this way, information from magnetic tape is encoded on a master disc;

Andreas Sofroniou

subsequently, the master is replicated by a process called stamping. In the read mode, low-intensity laser light is reflected off the disc surface and is "read" by light-sensitive diodes.

The radiant energy received by the diodes varies according to the presence of the pits, and this input is digitized by the diode circuits. The digital signals are then converted to analogue information on a video screen or in printout form.

Since the introduction of this technology, three main types of optical storage media have become available:

(1) Rewritable,

(2) Write-once read-many (WORM), and

(3) Compact disc read-only memory (CD-ROM).

Andreas Sofroniou

Rewritable discs are functionally equivalent to magnetic disks, although the former are slower. WORM discs are used as an archival storage medium to enter data once and retrieve it many times. CD-ROMs are the preferred medium for electronic distribution of digital libraries and software.

To raise storage capacity, optical discs are arranged into "jukeboxes" holding as many as 10 million pages of text or more than one terabyte (one trillion bytes) of image data.

The high storage capacities and random access of the magneto-optical, rewritable discs are particularly suited for storing multimedia information, in which text, image, and sound are combined.

Recording techniques

Digitally stored information is commonly referred to as data, and its analogue counterpart is called source data.

Vast quantities of non-document analogue data are collected, digitized, and compressed automatically by means of appropriate instruments in fields such as astronomy, environmental monitoring, scientific experimentation and modelling, and national security.

The capture of information generated by humankind, in the form of packages of symbols called documents, is accomplished by manual and, increasingly, automatic techniques.

Data are entered manually by striking the keys of a keyboard, touching a computer screen, or writing by hand on a digital tablet or its variant, the so-called pen computer.

Manual data entry, a slow and error-prone process, is facilitated to a degree by special computer programs that include editing software, with which to insert formatting commands, verify spelling, and make text changes, and document-formatting software, with which to arrange and rearrange text and graphics flexibly on the output page.

It is estimated that 5 percent of all documents in the United States exist in digitized form and that two-thirds of the paper documents cannot be digitized by keyboard transcription because they contain drawings or still images and because such transcription would be highly uneconomical.

Such documents are digitized economically by a process called document imaging.

Document imaging utilizes digital scanners to generate a digital representation of a document page. An image scanner divides the page into minute picture areas called pixels and produces an array of binary digits, each representing the brightness of a pixel.

The resulting stream of bits is enhanced and compressed (to as little as 10 percent of the original volume) by a device called an image controller and is stored on a magnetic or optical medium.

A large storage capacity is required, because it takes about 45,000 bytes to store a typical compressed text page of 2,500 characters and as much as 1,000,000 bytes to store a page containing an image.

Aside from document imaging applications, digital scanning is used for transmission of documents via facsimile, in satellite photography, and in other applications.

An image scanner digitizes an entire document page for storage and display as an image and does not recognize characters and words of text.

The stored material therefore cannot be linguistically manipulated by text processing and other software techniques.

When such manipulation is desired, a software program performs the optical character recognition (OCR) function by converting each optically scanned character into an electric signal and comparing it with the internally stored representation of an alphabet of characters, so as to select from it the one that matches the scanned character most closely or to reject it as an unidentifiable token.

The more sophisticated of present-day OCR programs distinguish shapes, sizes, and pitch of symbols—including handwriting—and learn from experience. A universal OCR machine is not available, however, for even a single alphabet.

Still photographs can be digitized by scanning or transferred from film to a compact digital disc holding more than 100 images. A recent development, the digital camera, makes it possible to bypass the film/paper step completely by capturing the image into the camera's random-access memory or a special diskette and then transferring it to a personal computer.

Since both technologies produce a graphics file, in either case the image is editable by means of suitable software.

The digital recording of sound is important because speech is the most frequently used natural carrier of communicable information.

Direct capture of sound into personal computers is accomplished by means of a digital signal processor (DSP) chip, a special-purpose device built into the computer to perform array-processing operations.

Conversion of analogue audio signals to digital recordings is a commonplace process that has been used for years by the telecommunications and entertainment industries.

Although the resulting digital sound track can be edited, automatic speech recognition—analogous to the recognition of characters and words in text by means of optical character recognition—is still under development.

When perfected, voice recognition is certain to have a tremendous impact on the way humans communicate with recorded information, with computers, and among themselves.

By the beginning of the 1990s, the technology to record (or convert), store in digital form, and edit all visually and aurally perceived signals—text, graphics, still images, animation, motion video, and sound—had thus become available and affordable.

These capabilities opened a way for a new kind of multimedia document that employs print, video, and sound to generate more powerful and colourful messages, communicate them securely at electronic speeds, and allow them to be modified almost at will.

The traditional business letter, newspaper, journal, and book will no longer be the same.

Inventory of recorded information

The development of recording media and techniques enabled society to begin building a store of human knowledge.

The idea of collecting and organizing written records is thought to have originated in Sumer about 5,000 years ago; Egyptian writing was introduced soon after.

Early collections of Sumerian and Egyptian writings recorded in cuneiform on clay tablets and in hieroglyphic script on papyrus, contained information about legal and economic transactions. In these and other early document collections (e.g., those of China produced during the Shang dynasty in the 2nd millennium BC and Buddhist collections in India dating to the 5th century BC), it is difficult to separate the concepts of the archive and the library.

From the Middle East the concept of document collections penetrated the Greco-Roman world. Roman kings institutionalized the population and property census as early as the 6th century BC.

The great Library of Alexandria, established in the 3rd century BC, is best known as a large collection of papyri containing inventories of property, taxes, and other payments by citizens to their rulers and to each other. It is, in short, the ancient equivalent of today's administrative information systems.

The scholarly splendour of the Islamic world from the 8th to the 13th century AD can in large part be attributed to the maintenance of public and private book libraries.

The Bayt al-Ḥikmah ("House of Wisdom"), founded in AD 830 in Baghdad, contained a public library with a large collection of materials on a wide range of subjects, and the 10th-century library of Caliph al-Ḥakam in Cordova, Spain, boasted more than 400,000 books.

Primary and secondary literature

The late but rapid development of European libraries from the 16th century on followed the invention of printing from movable type, which spurred the growth of the printing and publishing industries.

Since the beginning of the 17th century, literature has become the principal medium for disseminating knowledge.

The phrase primary literature is used to designate original information in various printed formats: newspapers, monographs, conference proceedings, learned and trade journals, reports, patents, bulletins, and newsletters.

The scholarly journal, the classic medium of scientific communication, first appeared in 1665.

Three hundred years later the number of periodical titles published in the world was estimated at more than 60,000, reflecting not only growth in the number of practitioners of science and expansion of its body of knowledge through specialization but also a maturing of the system of rewards that encourages scientists to publish.

The sheer quantity of printed information has for some time prevented any individual from fully absorbing even a minuscule fraction of it.

Such devices as tables of contents, summaries, and indexes of various types, which aid in identifying and locating relevant information in primary literature, have been in use since the 16th century and led to the development of what is termed secondary literature during the 19th century.

The purpose of secondary literature is to "filter" the primary information sources, usually by subject area, and provide the indicators to this literature in the form of reviews, abstracts, and indexes.

Over the past 100 years there has evolved a system of disciplinary, national, and international abstracting and indexing services that acts as a gateway to several attributes of primary literature: authors, subjects, publishers, dates (and languages) of publication, and citations.

The professional activity associated with these access-facilitating tools is called documentation.

The quantity of printed materials also makes it impossible, as well as undesirable, for any institution to acquire and house more than a small portion of it.

The husbanding of recorded information has become a matter of public policy, as many countries have established national libraries and archives to direct the orderly acquisition of analogue-form documents and records.

Since these institutions alone are not able to keep up with the output of such documents and records, new forms of cooperative planning and sharing recorded materials are evolving—namely, public and private, national and regional library networks and consortia.

Andreas Sofroniou

DATABASES

Bibliographic and numeric databases

The emergence of digital technology in the mid-20th century has affected humankind's inventory of recorded information dramatically.

During the early 1960s computers were used to digitize text for the first time; the purpose was to reduce the cost and time required to publish two American abstracting journals, the *Index Medicus* of the National Library of Medicine and the *Scientific and Technical Aerospace Reports* of the National Aeronautics and Space Administration (NASA).

By the late 1960s such bodies of digitized alphanumeric information, known as bibliographic and numeric databases, constituted a new type of information resource. This resource is husbanded outside the traditional repositories of information (libraries and archives) by database "vendors."

Advances in computer storage, telecommunications, software for computer sharing, and automated techniques of text indexing and searching fuelled the development of an on-line database service industry.

Meanwhile, electronic applications to bibliographic control in libraries and archives have led to the development of computerized catalogues and of union catalogs in library networks. They also have resulted in the introduction of comprehensive automation programs in these institutions.

The explosive growth of communications networks after 1990, particularly in the scholarly world, has accelerated the establishment of the "virtual library." At the leading edge of this development is public-domain information.

Residing in thousands of databases distributed worldwide, a growing portion of this vast resource is now accessible almost instantaneously via the Internet, the web of computer networks linking the global communities of researchers and, increasingly, non-academic organizations.

Internet resources of electronic information include selected library catalogues, collected works of the literature, some abstracting journals, full-text electronic journals, encyclopaedias, and scientific data from numerous disciplines, software archives, demographic registers, daily news summaries, environmental reports, and prices in commodity markets, as well as hundreds of thousands of e-mail and bulletin-board messages.

The vast inventory of recorded information can be useful only if it is systematically organized and if mechanisms exist for locating in it items relevant to human needs.

The main approaches for achieving such organization are reviewed in the following section, as are the tools used to retrieve desired information.

Organization and retrieval of information

In any collection, physical objects are related by order. The ordering may be random or according to some characteristic called a key. Such characteristics may be intrinsic properties of the objects (e.g., size, weight, shape, or colour), or they may be assigned from some agreed-upon set, such as object class or date of purchase.

The values of the key are arranged in a sorting sequence that is dependent on the

Andreas Sofroniou

type of key involved: alphanumeric key values are usually sorted in alphabetic sequence, while other types may be sorted on the basis of similarity in class, such as books on a particular subject or flora of the same genus.

In most cases, order is imposed on a set of information objects for two reasons: to create their inventory and to facilitate locating specific objects in the set.

There also exist other, secondary objectives for selecting a particular ordering, as, for example, conservation of space or economy of effort in fetching objects. Unless the objects in a collection are replicated, any ordering scheme is one-dimensional and unable to meet all the functions of ordering with equal effectiveness.

The main approach for overcoming some of the limitations of one-dimensional ordering of recorded information relies on extended description of its content and, for analogue-form information, of some features of the physical items. This approach employs various tools of content analysis that subsequently facilitate accessing and searching recorded information.

Description and content analysis of analogue-form records

The collections of libraries and archives, the primary repositories of analogue-form information, constitute one-dimensional ordering of physical materials in print (documents), in image form (maps and photographs), or in audio-video format (recordings and videotapes).

To break away from the confines of one-dimensional ordering, librarianship has developed an extensive set of attributes in terms of which it describes each item in the collection.

The rules for assigning these attributes are called cataloguing rules. Descriptive cataloguing is the extraction of bibliographic elements (author names, title, publisher, date of publication, etc.) from each item; the assignment of subject categories or headings to such items is termed subject cataloguing.

Conceptually, the library catalogue is a table or matrix in which each row describes a discrete physical item and each column provides values of the assigned key. When such a catalogue is represented digitally in a computer, any attribute can serve as the ordering key.

By sorting the catalogue on different keys, it is possible to produce a variety of indexes as well as subject bibliographies.

More important, any of the attributes of a computerized catalogue becomes a search key (access point) to the collection, surpassing the utility of the traditional card catalogue.

The most useful access key to analogue-form items is subject. The extensive lists of subject headings of library classification schemes provide, however, only a gross access tool to the content of the items. A technique called indexing provides a refinement over library subject headings.

It consists of extracting from the item or assigning to it subject and other "descriptors"—words or phrases denoting significant concepts (topics, names) that occur in or characterize the content of the record.

Indexing frequently accompanies abstracting, a technique for condensing the full text of a document into a short summary that contains its main ideas (but invariably incurs an information loss and often introduces a bias).

Computer-printed, indexed abstracting journals provide a means of keeping users informed of primary information sources.

Description and content analysis of digital-form information

The description of an electronic document generally follows the principles of bibliographic cataloguing if the document is part of a database that is expected to be accessed directly and individually.

When the database is an element of a universe of globally distributed database servers that are searchable in parallel, the matter of document naming is considerably more challenging, because several complexities are introduced.

Andreas Sofroniou

The document description must include the name of the database server—i.e., its physical location. Because database servers may delete particular documents, the description must also contain a pointer to the document's logical address (the generating organization).

In contrast to their usefulness in the descriptive cataloguing of analogue documents, physical attributes such as format and size are highly variable in the milieu of electronic documents and therefore are meaningless in a universal document-naming scheme.

On the other hand, the data type of the document (text, sound, etc.) is critical to its transmission and use. Perhaps the most challenging design is the "living document"— a constantly changing pastiche consisting of sections electronically copied from different documents, interspersed with original narrative or graphics or voice comments contributed by persons in distant locations, whose different versions reside on different servers.

Efforts are under way to standardize the naming of documents in the universe of electronic networks.

Machine indexing

The subject analysis of electronic text is accomplished by means of machine indexing, using one of two approaches: the assignment of subject descriptors from an unlimited vocabulary (free indexing) or their assignment from a list of authorized descriptors (controlled indexing).

A collection of authorized descriptors is called an authority list or, if it also displays various relationships among descriptors such as hierarchy or synonymy, a thesaurus.

The result of the indexing process is a computer file known as an inverted index, which is an alphabetic listing of descriptors and the addresses of their occurrence in the document body.

Full-text indexing, the use of every character string (word of a natural language) in the text as an index term, is an extreme case of free-text indexing: each word in the document (except function words such as articles and prepositions) becomes an access point to it.

Used earlier for the generation of concordances in literary analysis and other computer applications in the humanities, full-text indexing placed great demands on computer storage because the resulting index is at least as large as the body of the text.

With decreasing cost of mass storage, automatic full-text indexing capability has been incorporated routinely into state-of-the-art information-management software.

Text indexing may be supplemented by other syntactic techniques so as to increase its precision or robustness. One such method, the Standard Generalized Markup Language (SGML), takes advantage of standard text markers used by editors to pinpoint the location and other characteristics of document elements (paragraphs and tables, for example).

In indexing spatial data such as maps and astronomical images, the textual index specifies the search areas, each of which is further described by a set of coordinates defining a rectangle or irregular polygon.

These digital spatial document attributes are then used to retrieve and display a specific point or a selected region of the document.

There are other specialized techniques that may be employed to augment the indexing of specific document types, such as encyclopaedias, electronic mail, catalogs, bulletin boards, tables, and maps.

Semantic content analysis

The analysis of digitally recorded natural-language information from the semantic viewpoint is a matter of considerable complexity, and it lies at the foundation of such incipient applications as automatic question answering from a database or retrieval by means of unrestricted natural-language queries.

The general approach has been that of computational linguistics: to derive representations of the syntactic and semantic relations between the linguistic elements of sentences and larger parts of the document.

Syntactic relations are described by parsing (decomposing) the grammar of sentences.

For semantic representation, three related formalisms dominate. In a so-called semantic network, conceptual entities such as objects, actions, or events are represented as a graph of linked nodes. "Frames" represent, in a similar graph network, physical or abstract attributes of objects and in a sense define the objects. In "scripts," events and actions rather than objects are defined in terms of their attributes.

Indexing and linguistic analyses of text generate a relatively gross measure of the semantic relationship, or subject similarity, of documents in a given collection. Subject similarity is, however, a pragmatic phenomenon that varies with the observer and the circumstances of an observation (purpose, time, and so forth).

A technique experimented with briefly in the mid-1960s, which assigned to each document one or more "roles" (functions) and one or more "links" (pointers to other documents having the same or a similar role), showed potential for a pragmatic measure of similarity; its use, however, was too unwieldy for the computing environment of the day.

Some 20 years later, a similar technique became popular under the name "hypertext." In this technique, documents that a person or a group of persons consider related (by concept, sequence, hierarchy, experience, motive, or other characteristics) are connected via "hyperlinks," mimicking the way humans associate ideas.

Objects so linked need not be only text; speech and music, graphics and images, and animation and video can all be interlinked into a "hypermedia" database.

Andreas Sofroniou

The objects are stored with their hyperlinks, and a user can easily navigate the network of associations by clicking with a mouse on a series of entries on a computer screen. Another technique that elicits semantic relationships from a body of text is SGML.

Image analysis

The content analysis of images is accomplished by two primary methods: image processing and pattern recognition. Image processing is a set of computational techniques for analyzing, enhancing, compressing, and reconstructing images. Pattern recognition is an information-reduction process: the assignment of visual or logical patterns to classes based on the features of these patterns and their relationships.

The stages in pattern recognition involve measurement of the object to identify distinguishing attributes, extraction of features for the defining attributes, and assignment of the object to a class based on these features. Both image processing and pattern recognition have extensive applications in various areas, including astronomy, medicine, industrial robotics, and remote sensing by satellites.

Speech analysis

The immediate objective of content analysis of digital speech is the conversion of discrete sound elements into their alphanumeric equivalents. Once so represented, speech can be subjected to the same techniques of content analysis as natural-language text— i.e., indexing and linguistic analysis.

Andreas Sofroniou

Converting speech elements into their alphanumeric counterparts is an intriguing problem because the "shape" of speech sounds embodies a wide range of many acoustic characteristics and because the linguistic elements of speech are not clearly distinguishable from one another.

The technique used in speech processing is to classify the spectral representations of sound and to match the resulting digital spectrographs against pre-stored "templates" so as to identify the alphanumeric equivalent of the sound. (The obverse of this technique, the digital-to-analogue conversion of such templates into sound, is a relatively straightforward approach to generating synthetic speech.)

Speech processing is complex as well as expensive in terms of storage capacity and computational requirements. State-of-the-art speech recognition systems can identify

Andreas Sofroniou

limited vocabularies and parts of distinctly spoken speech and can be programmed to recognize tonal idiosyncrasies of individual speakers.

When more robust and reliable techniques become available and the process is made computationally tractable (as is expected with parallel computers), humans will be able to interact with computers via spoken commands and queries on a routine basis. In many situations this may make the keyboard obsolete as a data-entry device.

Storage structures for digital-form information

Digital information is stored in complex patterns that make it feasible to address and operate on even the smallest element of symbolic expression, as well as on larger strings such as words or sentences and on images and sound.

From the viewpoint of digital information storage, it is useful to distinguish between "structured" data, such as inventories of objects that can be represented by short symbol strings and numbers, and "unstructured" data, such as the natural-language text of documents or pictorial images. The principal objective of all storage structures is to facilitate the processing of data elements on the basis of their relationships; the structures thus vary with the type of relationship they represent.

The choice of a particular storage structure is governed by the relevance of the relationships it allows to be represented to the information-processing requirements of the task or system at hand.

In information systems whose store consists of unstructured databases of natural-language records, the objective is to retrieve records (or portions thereof) on the basis of the presence in the records of words or short phrases that constitute the query.

Since there exists an index as a separate file that provides information about the locations of words and phrases in the database records, the relationships that are of interest (e.g., word adjacency) can be calculated from the index.

Consequently, the database text itself can be stored as a simple ordered sequential file of records. The majority of the computations use the index, and they access the text file only to pull out the records or those portions that satisfy the result of the computations.

The sequential file structure remains popular, with document-retrieval software intended for use with personal computers and CD-ROM databases.

When relationships between data elements need to be represented as part of the records so as to make more efficient the desired operations on these records, two types of "chained" structures are commonly used: hierarchical and network.

In the hierarchical file structure, records are arranged in a scheme resembling a family tree, with records related to one another from top to bottom. In the network file structure, records are arranged in groupings known as sets; these can be connected in any number of ways, giving rise to considerable flexibility.

In both hierarchical and network structures, the relationships are shown by means of "pointers" (i.e., identifiers such as addresses or keys) that become part of the records.

Another type of database storage structure, the relational structure, has become increasingly popular since the late 1970s.

Its major advantage over the hierarchical and network structures is the ability to handle unanticipated data relationships without pointers.

Relational storage structures are two-dimensional tables consisting of rows and columns, much like the conceptual library catalogue mentioned above.

The elegance of the relational model lies in its conceptual simplicity, the availability of theoretical underpinnings (relational algebra), and the ability of its associated software to handle data relationships without the use of pointers.

The relational model was initially used for databases containing highly structured information. In the 1990s it largely replaced the hierarchical and network models, and it also became the model of choice for large-scale information-management applications, both textual and multimedia.

The feasibility of storing large volumes of full text on an economical medium (the digital optical disc) has renewed interest in the study of storage structures that permit more powerful retrieval and processing techniques to operate on cognitive entities other than words, to facilitate more extensive semantic content and context analysis, and to organize text conceptually into logical units rather than those dictated by printing conventions.

Query languages

The uses of databases are manifold. They provide a means of retrieving records or parts of records and performing various calculations before displaying the results.

The interface by which such manipulations are specified is called the query language.

Whereas early query languages were originally so complex that interacting with electronic databases could be done only by specially trained individuals, recent interfaces are more user-friendly, allowing casual users to access database information.

The main types of popular query modes are the menu, the "fill-in-the-blank" technique, and the structured query. Particularly suited for novices, the menu requires a person to choose from several alternatives displayed on the video terminal screen.

The fill-in-the-blank technique is one in which the user is prompted to enter key words as search statements.

The structured query approach is effective with relational databases. It has a formal, powerful syntax that is in fact a programming language, and it is able to accommodate logical operators. One implementation of this approach, the Structured Query Language (SQL), has the form

- *Select* [field Fa, Fb, . . . , Fn]

- *From* [database Da, Db, . . . , Dn]

- *Where* [field Fa = abc] *and* [field Fb = def].

Structured query languages support database searching and other operations by using commands such as "find," "delete," "print," "sum," and so forth.

The sentence-like structure of an SQL query resembles natural language except that its syntax is limited and fixed. Instead of using an SQL statement, it is possible to represent queries in tabular form.

The technique, referred to as query-by-example (or QBE), displays an empty tabular form and expects the searcher to enter the search specifications into appropriate columns. The program then constructs an SQL-type query from the table and executes it.

The most flexible query language is of course natural language. The use of natural-language sentences in a constrained form to search databases is allowed by some commercial database management software.

These programs parse the syntax of the query; recognize its action words and their synonyms; identify the names of files, records, and fields; and perform the logical operations required.

Experimental systems that accept such natural-language queries in spoken voice have been developed; however, the ability to employ unrestricted natural language to query unstructured information will require further advances in machine understanding of

Andreas Sofroniou

natural language, particularly in techniques of representing the semantic and pragmatic context of ideas.

The prospect of an intelligent conversation between humans and a large store of digitally encoded knowledge is not imminent.

Information searching and retrieval

State-of-the-art approaches to retrieving information employ two generic techniques:

(1) Matching words in the query against the database index (key-word searching) and

(2) Traversing the database with the aid of hypertext or hypermedia links.

Key-word searches can be made either more general or more narrow in scope by means of logical operators (e.g., disjunction and conjunction). Because of the semantic ambiguities involved in free-text indexing,

Andreas Sofroniou

however, the precision of the key-word retrieval technique—that is, the percentage of relevant documents correctly retrieved from a collection—is far from ideal, and various modifications have been introduced to improve it.

In one such enhancement, the search output is sorted by degree of relevance, based on a statistical match between the key words in the query and in the document; in another, the program automatically generates a new query using one or more documents considered relevant by the user. Key-word searching has been the dominant approach to text retrieval since the early 1960s; hypertext has so far been largely confined to personal or corporate information-retrieval applications.

The exponential growth of the use of computer networks in the 1990s presages significant changes in systems and techniques of information retrieval. In a wide-

243

area information service, a number of which began operating at the beginning of the 1990s on the Internet computer network, a user's personal computer or terminal (called a client) can search simultaneously a number of databases maintained on heterogeneous computers (called servers).

The latter are located at different geographic sites, and their databases contain different data types and often use incompatible data formats. The simultaneous, distributed search is possible because clients and servers agree on a standard document addressing scheme and adopt a common communications protocol that accommodates all the data types and formats used by the servers.

Communication with other wide-area services using different protocols is accomplished by routing through so-called gateways capable of protocol translation.

Several representative clients are shown: a "dumb" terminal (i.e., one with no internal processor), a personal computer (PC), a Macintosh (Mac), and a NeXT machine. They have access to data on the servers sharing a common protocol as well as to data provided by services that require protocol conversion via the gateways. Network news is such a wide-area service, containing hundreds of news groups on a variety of subjects, by which users can read and post messages.

Evolving information-retrieval techniques, exemplified by an experimental interface to the NASA space shuttle reference manual, combine natural language, hyperlinks, and key-word searching. Other techniques, seeking higher levels of retrieval precision and effectiveness, are studied by researchers involved with artificial intelligence and neural networks.

The next major milestone may be a computer program that traverses the seamless information universe of wide-area electronic networks and continuously filters its contents through profiles of organizational and personal interest: the information robot of the 21st century.

Information display

For humans to perceive and understand information, it must be presented as print and image on paper; as print and image on film or on a video terminal; as sound via radio or telephony; as print, sound, and video in motion pictures, on television broadcasts, or at lectures and conferences; or in face-to-face encounters.

Except for live encounters and audio information, such displays emanate increasingly from digitally stored data, with

Andreas Sofroniou

the output media being video, print, and sound.

Video

Possibly the most widely used video display device, at least in the industrialized world, is the television set. Designed primarily for video and sound, its image resolution is inadequate for alphanumeric data except in relatively small amounts.

Use of the television set in text-oriented information systems has been limited to menu-oriented applications such as videotex, in which information is selected from hierarchically arranged menus (with the aid of a numeric keyboard attachment) and displayed in fixed frames.

The television, computer, and communications technologies are, however, converging in a high-resolution digital

Andreas Sofroniou

television set capable of receiving alphanumeric, video, and audio signals.

The computer video terminal is today's ubiquitous interface that transforms computer-stored data into analogue form for human viewing. The two basic apparatuses used are the cathode-ray tube (CRT) and the more recent flat-panel display.

In CRT displays an electron gun emits beams of electrons on a phosphorus-coated surface; the beams are deflected, forming visible patterns representative of data. Flat-panel displays use one of four different media for visual representation of data: liquid crystal, light-emitting diodes, plasma panels, and electroluminescence.

Advanced video display systems enable the user to scroll, page, zoom (change the scale of the details of the display image for enhancement), divide the screen into multiple colours and windows (viewing areas), and in some cases even activate commands by touching the screen instead of using the keyboard.

The information capacity of the terminal screen depends on its resolution, which ranges from low (character-addressable) to high (bit-addressable).

High resolution is indispensable for the display of graphic and video data in state-of-the-art workstations, such as those used in engineering or information systems design.

Print

Modern society continues to be dominated by printed information. The convenience and portability of print on paper make it difficult to imagine the paperless world that some have predicted.

The generation of paper print has changed considerably, however.

Although manual typesetting is still practiced for artwork, in special situations, and in some developing countries, electronic means of composing pages for subsequent reproduction by photo-duplication and other methods has become commonplace.

Since the 1960s, volume publishing has become an automated process using large computers and high-speed printers to transfer digitally stored data on paper. The appearance of microcomputer-based publishing systems has proved to be another significant advance.

Economical enough to allow even small organizations to become in-house publishers, these so-called desktop publishing systems are able to format text and graphics interactively on a high-resolution video screen with the aid of page-description command languages.

Once a page has been formatted, the entire image is transferred to an electronic printing or photocomposition device.

Printers

Computer printers are commonly divided into two general classes according to the way they produce images on paper: impact and non-impact. In the first type, images are formed by the print mechanism making contact with the paper through an ink-coated ribbon.

The mechanism consists either of print hammers shaped like characters or of a print head containing a row of pins that produce a pattern of dots in the form of characters or other images.

Most non-impact printers form images from a matrix of dots, but they employ different techniques for transferring images to paper.

The most popular type, the laser printer, uses a beam of laser light and a system of optical components to etch images on a photoconductor drum from which they are carried via electrostatic photocopying to paper.

Light-emitting diode (LED) printers resemble laser printers in operation but direct light from energized diodes rather than a laser onto a photoconductive surface. Ion-deposition printers make use of technology similar to that of photocopiers for producing electrostatic images.

Another type of non-impact printer, the ink-jet printer, sprays electrically charged drops of ink onto the print surface.

Microfilm and microfiche

Alphanumeric and image information can be transferred from digital computer storage directly to film.

Reel microfilm and microfiche (a flat sheet of film containing multiple micro-images reduced from the original) were popular methods of document storage and reproduction for several decades.

During the 1990s they were largely replaced by optical disc technology.

Voice

In synthetic speech generation, digitally pre-stored sound elements are converted to analogue sound signals and combined to form words and sentences.

Digital-to-analogue converters are available as inexpensive boards for microcomputers or as software for larger machines.

Human speech is the most effective natural form of communication, and so applications of this technology are becoming increasingly popular in situations where there are numerous requests for specific information (e.g., time, travel, and entertainment), where there is a need for repetitive instruction, in electronic voice mail (the counterpart of electronic text mail), and in toys.

Dissemination of information

The process of recording information by handwriting was obviously laborious and required the dedication of the likes of Egyptian scribes or monks in monasteries around the world. It was only after mechanical means of reproducing writing were invented that information records could be duplicated more efficiently and economically.

The first practical method of reproducing writing mechanically was block printing; it was developed in China during the T'ang dynasty (618–907).

Ideographic text and illustrations were engraved in wooden blocks, inked, and copied on paper. Used to produce books as well as cards, charms, and calendars, block printing spread to Korea and Japan but apparently not to the Islamic or European Christian civilizations.

European woodcuts and metal engravings date only to the 14th century.

Printing from movable type was also invented in China (in the mid-11th century AD). There and in the bookmaking industry of Korea, where the method was applied more extensively during the 15th century, the ideographic type was made initially of baked clay and wood and later of metal.

The large number of typefaces required for pictographic text composition continued to handicap printing in the Orient until the present time.

The invention of character-oriented printing from movable type (1440–50) is attributed to the German printer Johannes Gutenberg. Within 30 years of his invention, the movable-type printing press was in use throughout Europe.

Character-type pieces were metallic and apparently cast from metallic molds; paper and vellum (calfskin parchment) were used to carry the impressions.

Gutenberg's technique of assembling individual letters by hand was employed until 1886, when the German-born American printer Ottmar Mergenthaler developed the Linotype, a keyboard-driven device that cast lines of type automatically.

Typesetting speed was further enhanced by the Monotype technique, in which a perforated paper ribbon, punched from a keyboard, was used to operate a type-casting machine.

Mechanical methods of typesetting prevailed until the 1960s. Since that time they have been largely supplanted by the electronic and optical printing techniques described in the previous section.

Unlike the use of movable type for printing text, early graphics were reproduced from wood relief engravings in which the nonprinting portions of the image were cut away. Musical scores, on the other hand, were reproduced from etched stone plates.

At the end of the 18th century, the German printer Aloys Senefelder developed lithography, a plano-graphic technique of transferring images from a specially prepared surface of stone. In offset lithography the image is transferred from zinc or aluminium plates instead of stone, and in photoengraving such plates are superimposed with film and then etched.

The first successful photographic process, the daguerreotype, was developed during the 1830s.

The invention of photography, aside from providing a new medium for capturing still images and later video in analogue form, was significant for two other reasons.

First, recorded information (textual and graphic) could be easily reproduced from film, and, second, the image could be enlarged or reduced.

Document reproduction from film to film has been relatively unimportant, because both printing and photocopying (see above) are cheaper.

The ability to reduce images, however, has led to the development of the microform, the most economical method of disseminating analogue-form information.

Another technique of considerable commercial importance for the duplication of paper-based information is photocopying, or dry photography.

Printing is most economical when large numbers of copies are required, but photocopying provides a fast and efficient means of duplicating records in small quantities for personal or local use.

Of the several technologies that are in use, the most popular process, xerography, is based on electrostatics. While the volume of information issued in the form of printed matter continues unabated, the electronic publishing industry has begun to disseminate information in digital form. The digital optical disc is developing as an increasingly popular means of issuing large bodies of archival information—for example, legislation, court and hospital records, encyclopaedias and other reference works, referral databases, and libraries of computer software.

Full-text databases, each containing digital page images of the complete text of some 400 periodicals stored on CD-ROM, entered the market in 1990.

The optical disc provides the mass production technology for publication in machine-readable form. It offers the prospect of having large libraries of information available in virtually every school and at many professional workstations. The coupling of computers and digital telecommunications is also changing the modes of information dissemination.

High-speed digital satellite communications facilitate electronic printing at remote sites; for example, the world's major newspapers and magazines transmit electronic page copies to different geographic locations for local printing and distribution.

Updates of catalogues, computer software, and archival databases are distributed via e-mail, a method of rapidly forwarding and storing bodies of digital information between remote computers.

Indeed, a large-scale transformation is taking place in modes of formal as well as informal communication. For more than three centuries, formal communication in the scientific community has relied on the scholarly and professional periodical, widely distributed to tens of thousands of libraries and to tens of millions of individual subscribers.

In 1992 a major international publisher announced that its journals would gradually be available for computer storage in digital form; and in that same year the State University of New York at Buffalo began building a completely electronic, paperless library.

The scholarly article, rather than the journal, is likely to become the basic unit of formal communication in scientific disciplines; digital copies of such an article will be transmitted electronically to subscribers or, more likely, on demand to individuals and organizations who learn of its existence through referral databases and new types of alerting information services.

The Internet already offers instantaneous public access to vast resources of non-commercial information stored in computers around the world.

Similarly, the traditional modes of informal communications—various types of face-to-face encounters such as meetings, conferences, seminars, workshops, and classroom lectures—are being supplemented and in some cases replaced by e-mail, electronic bulletin boards (a technique of broadcasting newsworthy textual and multimedia messages between computer users), and electronic teleconferencing and distributed problem-solving (a method of linking remote persons in real time by voice-and-image communication and special software called "groupware").

These technologies are forging virtual societal networks—communities of geographically dispersed individuals who have common professional or social interests.

AUTOMATION, HISTORY OF

Technological concepts

The term *Automation* is now synonymous with all technological concepts; for the use and development of automatic machinery and systems, particularly those manufacturing or data-processing systems which require little or no human intervention in their normal operation.

Although the term was first used in 1946 to describe machinery being developed by the Ford Motor Company to move automobile components and work-pieces automatically to and from other machines, the origins of the concept are much older.

Andreas Sofroniou

During the 19th century a number of machines such as looms and lathes became increasingly self-regulating.

At the same time transfer-machines were developed, whereby a series of machine-tools, each doing one operation automatically, became linked in a continuous production line by pneumatic or hydraulic devices transferring components from one operation to the next.

In addition to these technological advances in automation, the theory of 'scientific management', which was based on the early time-and-motion studies of Frederick Winslow Taylor in Philadelphia, USA, in the 1880s was designed by Taylor to enhance the efficiency and productivity of workers and machines.

In the early 20th century, with the development of electrical devices and time-switches, more processes became automatically controlled, and a number of basic industries such as oil-refining, chemicals, and food-processing were increasingly automated.

The development of computers after World War II enabled more sophisticated automation to be used in manufacturing industries, for example in iron and steel production.

The most familiar example of a highly automated system is perhaps an assembly plant for automobiles or other complex products.

Such a plant might involve the automatic machining, welding, transfer, and assembly of parts, using equipment and techniques such as numerically controlled machine-tools, automatically controlled robot arms, and guided vehicles, automated warehousing, materials handling, stock control, and so on.

Andreas Sofroniou

Advances in automation have been the result of a combination of many factors, including:

1. Modifications to the physical layout of production or processing facilities to ease handling;

2. Improvements in materials to facilitate manufacturing processes;

3. increasing mechanization of individual processes (the carrying out of tasks by machine rather than human actions), which often necessitates changes to the processes themselves;

4. Changes in product design to aid mechanization and mass production;

5. more advanced instrumentation and control systems for both individual machines and for plants as a whole; and

6. The adoption of information technology as an integral part of the production

process, leading ultimately to the concept of computer-integrated manufacturing.

Over the last few decades automation has evolved from the comparatively straightforward mechanization of tasks traditionally carried out by hand, through the introduction of complex automatic control systems, to the widespread automation of information collection and processing.

Whereas in the past automation has involved a high degree of standardization and uniformity in production, the increasing use of information technology has now made it possible to develop more flexible manufacturing systems.

HUMAN COMPUTER INTEGRATION

Integrating sciences

It is hoped that the following diagram will prompt more inclusions and thoughts in the COMPUTER PROGRAMS of the future.

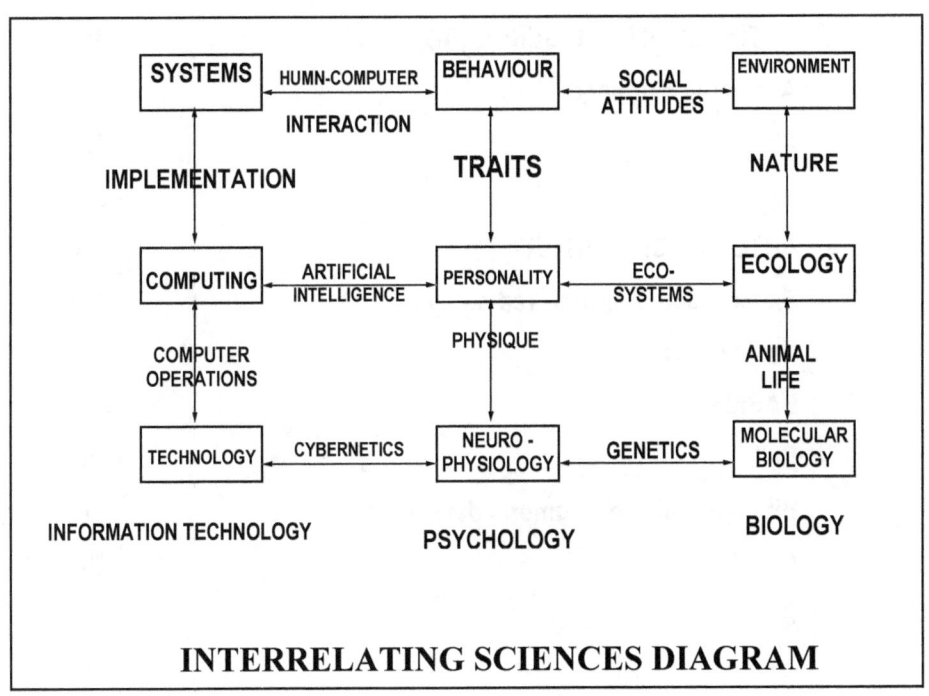

INTERRELATING SCIENCES DIAGRAM

END

Andreas Sofroniou

INDEX PAGE

Andreas Sofroniou

Andreas Sofroniou

Andreas Sofroniou

Andreas Sofroniou

Andreas Sofroniou

Andreas Sofroniou

BIBLIOGRAPHY

ALL BOOKS LISTED BELOW ARE PUBLISHED BY ANDREAS SOFRONIOU

1. THERAPEUTIC PSYCHOLOGY, ISBN: 978-1-326-34523-5

2. MEDICAL ETHICS THROUGH THE AGES, ISBN: 978-1-4092- 7468-1

3. MEDICAL ETHICS, FROM HIPPOCRATES TO THE 21ST CENTURY ISBN: 978-1-4457-1203-1

4. MISINTERPRETATION OF SIGMUND FREUD, ISBN: 978-1-4467-1659-5

5. JUNG'S PSYCHOTHERAPY: THE PSYCHOLOGICAL & MYTHOLOGICAL METHODS, ISBN: 978-1-4477-4740-6

6. FREUDIAN ANALYSIS & JUNGIAN SYNTHESIS, ISBN: 978-1-4477-5996-6

7. ADLER'S INDIVIDUAL PSYCHOLOGY AND RELATED METHODS, ISBN: 978-1-291-85951-5

8. ADLERIAN INDIVIDUALISM , JUNGIAN SYNTHESIS, FREUDIAN ANALYSIS, ISBN: 978-1-291-85937-9

9. PSYCHOTHERAPY, CONCEPTS OF TREATMENT, ISBN: 978-1-291-50178-0

10. PSYCHOLOGY, CONCEPTS OF BEHAVIOUR, ISBN: 978-1-291-47573-9

11. PHILOSOPHY FOR HUMAN BEHAVIOUR, ISBN: 978-1-291-12707-2

12. SEX, AN EXPLORATION OF SEXUALITY, EROS AND LOVE, ISBN: 978-1-291-56931-5

13. PSYCHOLOGY FROM CONCEPTION TO SENILITY, ISBN: 978-1-4092-7218-2

14. PSYCHOLOGY OF CHILD CULTURE, ISBN: 978-1-4092-7619-7

15. JOYFUL PARENTING, ISBN: 0 9527956 1 2

16. GUIDE TO A JOYFUL PARENTING, ISBN: 0 952 7956 1 2

17. THERAPEUTIC PHILOSOPHY FOR THE INDIVIDUAL AND THE STATE, ISBN: 978-1-4092-7586-2

18. PHILOSOPHIC COUNSELLING FOR PEOPLE AND THEIR GOVERNMENTS, ISBN: 978-1-4092-7400-1

19. CHILD PSYCHOTHERAPY, ISBN: 978-1-326-44169-2

20. HYPNOTHERAPY IN MEDICINE, PSYCHOLOGY, MAGIC, ISBN: 978-1-326-48163-6

21. ART FOR PSYCHOTHERAPY, ISBN: 978-1-326-78959-6

22. SLEEPING AND DREAMING EXPLAINED BY ARTS & SCIENCE, ISBN: ISBN: 978-1-326-81309-3

23. PHILOSOPHY AND POLITICS, ISBN: 978-1-326-33854-1

24. MORAL PHILOSOPHY, FROM SOCRATES TO THE 21ST AEON, ISBN: 978-1-4457-4618-0

25. MORAL PHILOSOPHY, FROM HIPPOCRATES TO THE 21ST AEON, ISBN: 978-1-84753-463-7

26. MORAL PHILOSOPHY, THE ETHICAL APPROACH THROUGH THE AGES, ISBN: 978-1-4092-7703-3

27. MORAL PHILOSOPHY, ISBN: 978-1-4478-5037-3

28. 2011 POLITICS, ORGANISATIONS, PSYCHOANALYSIS, POETRY, ISBN: 978-1-4467-2741-6

29. WISDOM AN ACCUMULATION OF KNOWLEDGE, ISBN: 978-1-326-99692-5

Andreas Sofroniou

30. MYTHOLOGY LEGENDS FROM AROUND THE GLOBE, ISBN: 978-1-326-98630-8

31. PLATO'S EPISTEMOLOGY, ISBN: 978-1-4716-6584-4

32. ARISTOTLE'S AETIOLOGY, ISBN: 978-1-4716-7861-5

33. MARXISM, SOCIALISM & COMMUNISM, ISBN: 978-1-4716-8236-0

34. MACHIAVELLI'S POLITICS & RELEVANT PHILOSOPHICAL CONCEPTS, ISBN: 978-1-4716-8629-0

35. BRITISH PHILOSOPHERS, 16TH TO 18TH CENTURY, ISBN: 978-1-4717-1072-8

36. ROUSSEAU ON WILL AND MORALITY, ISBN: 978-1-4717-1070-4

37. EPISTEMOLOGY, A SYSTEMATIC OVERVIEW, ISBN: 978-1-326-11380-3

38. HEGEL ON IDEALISM, KNOWLEDGE & REALITY, ISBN: 978-1-4717-0954-8

39. METAPHYSICS FACTS AND FALLACIES, ISBN: 978-1-326-80745-0

40. SOCIAL SCIENCES AND PHILOLOGY, ISBN: 978-1-326-33840-4

41. PHILOLOGY, CONCEPTS OF EUROPEAN LITERATURE, ISBN: 978-1-291-49148-7

42. THREE MILLENNIA OF HELLENIC PHILOLOGY, ISBN: 978-1-291-49799-1

43. CYPRUS, PERMANENT DEPRIVATION OF FREEDOM, ISBN: 978-1-291-50833-8

44. SOCIOLOGY, CONCEPTS OF GROUP BEHAVIOUR, ISBN: 978-1-291-

Andreas Sofroniou

51888-7

45. SOCIAL SCIENCES, CONCEPTS OF BRANCHES AND RELATIONSHIPS ISBN: 978-1-291-52321-8

46. CONCEPTS OF SOCIAL SCIENTISTS AND GREAT THINKERS, ISBN: 978-1-291-53786-4

47. EMPIRES AND COLONIALISM ISBN: 978-1-326-46761-6

48. CYPRUS, COLONISED BY MOST EMPIRES, ISBN, 978-1-326-47164-4

49. PERICLES, GOLDEN AGE OF ATHENS, ISBN: 978-1-326-47592-5

50. TRIANGLE OF EDUCATION TRAINING EXPERIENCE, ISBN: 978-1-326-82934-6

51. HARMONY IS LOVE FRIENDSHIP SEX, ISBN: 978-1-326-85687-8

52. INTERNATIONAL HUMAN RIGHTS, ISBN: 978-1-326-87348-6

53. ANALYSIS OF LOGIC AND SANITY, ISBN: ISBN: 978-1-326-90604-7

54. INTERNATIONAL LAW, GLOBAL RELATIONS, WORLD POWERS, ISBN: 978-1-326-92921-3

55. MANAGEMENT SCIENCE AND BUSINESS, ISBN: 978-1-326-45508-8

56. ECONOMICS WORLD HOUSE RULES, ISBN: 978-1-326-96162-6

57. POLITICAL SYSTEMS NORMS AND LAWS, ISBN: 978-1-326-97404-6

58. HISTORY OF SYSTEMS, ENGINEERING, TECHNOLOGY, ISBN: 978-1-326-94420-9

59. INFORMATION TECHNOLOGY AND MANAGEMENT, ISBN: 978-1-326-34496-2

60. I.T. RISK MANAGEMENT, ISBN: 978-1-4467-5653-9

61. SYSTEMS ENGINEERING, ISBN: 978-1-4477-7553-9

62. BUSINESS INFORMATION SYSTEMS, CONCEPTS AND EXAMPLES, ISBN: 978-1-4092-7338-7

63. A GUIDE TO INFORMATION TECHNOLOGY, ISBN: 978-1-4092-7608-1

64. CHANGE MANAGEMENT IN I.T., ISBN: 978-1-4092-7712-5

65. FRONT-END DESIGN AND DEVELOPMENT FOR SYSTEMS APPLICATIONS, ISBN: 978-1-4092-7588-6

66. I.T RISK MANAGEMENT, ISBN: 978-1-4092-7488-9

67. I.T. RISK MANAGEMENT – 2011 EDITION, ISBN: 978-1-4467- 5653-9

68. SIMPLIFIED PROCEDURES FOR I.T. PROJECTS DEVELOPMENT, ISBN: 978-1-4092-7562-6

69. SIGMA METHODOLOGY FOR RISK MANAGEMENT IN SYSTEMS DEVELOPMENT, ISBN: 978-1-4092-7690-6

70. TRADING ON THE INTERNET IN THE YEAR 2000 AND BEYOND, ISBN: 978-1-4092- 7577

71. STRUCTURED SYSTEMS METHODOLOGY, ISBN: 978-1-4477-6610-0

72. INFORMATION TECHNOLOGY LOGICAL ANALYSIS, ISBN: 978-1-4717-1688-1

73. I.T. RISKS LOGICAL ANALYSIS, ISBN: 978-1-4717-1957-8

74. LOGICAL ANALYSIS OF I.T. CHANGES, ISBN: 978-1-4717-2288-2

75. LOGICAL ANALYSIS OF SYSTEMS, RISKS , CHANGES, ISBN: 978-1-4717-2294-3

76. COMPUTING, A PRÉCIS ON SYSTEMS, SOFTWARE AND HARDWARE, ISBN: 978-1-2910-5102-5

Andreas Sofroniou

77.   MANAGE THAT I.T. PROJECT, ISBN: 978-1-4717-5304-6

78.   CHANGE MANAGEMENT, ISBN: 978-1-4457-6114-5

79.   MANAGEMENT OF COMMERCIAL COMPUTING, ISBN: 978-1-4092-7550-3

80.   PROGRAMME MANAGEMENT WORKSHOP, ISBN: 978-1-4092-7583-1

81.   MANAGEMENT OF I.T. CHANGES, RISKS, WORKSHOPS, EPISTEMOLOGY, ISBN: 978-1-84753-147-6

82.   THE PHILOSOPHICAL CONCEPTS OF MANAGEMENT THROUGH THE AGES, ISBN: 978-1-4092- 7554-1

83.   MANAGEMENT OF PROJECTS, SYSTEMS, INTERNET, AND RISKS, ISBN: 978-1-4092- 7464-3

84.   HOW TO CONSTRUCT YOUR RESUMÊ, ISBN: 978-1-4092-7383-7

85.   DEFINE THAT SYSTEM, ISBN: 978-1-291-15094-0

86.   INFORMATION TECHNOLOGY WORKSHOP, ISBN: 978-1-291-16440-4

87.   CHANGE MANAGEMENT IN SYSTEMS, ISBN: 978-1-4457-1099-0

88.   SYSTEMS MANAGEMENT, ISBN: 978-1-4710-4907-1

89.   TECHNOLOGY, A STUDY OF MECHANICAL ARTS AND APPLIED SCIENCES, ISBN: 978-1-291-58550-6

90.   EXPERT SYSTEMS, KNOWLEDGE ENGINEERING FOR HUMAN REPLICATION, ISBN: 978-1-291- 59509-3

91.   ARTIFICIAL INTELLIGENCE AND INFORMATION TECHNOLOGY, ISBN: 978-1-291- 60445-0

92.   PROJECT MANAGEMENT PROCEDURES FOR SYSTEMS DEVELOPMENT, ISBN: 978-0-952-72531-2

Andreas Sofroniou

93. SURFING THE INTERNET, THEN, NOW, LATER. ISBN: 978-1--291-77653-9

94. ANALYTICAL DIAGRAMS FOR I.T. SYSTEMS, ISBN: 978-1-326-05786-2

95. INTEGRATION OF INFORMATION TECHNOLOGY, ISBN: 978-1-312-64303-1

96. TRAINING FOR CHANGES IN I.T. ISBN: 978-1-326-14325-1

97. WORKSHOP FOR PROJECTS MANAGEMENT, ISBN: 978-1-326-16162-0

98. SOFRONIOU COLLECTION OF FICTION BOOKS, ISBN: 978-1-326-07629-0

99. THE TOWERING MISFEASANCE, ISBN: 978-1-4241-3652-0

100. DANCES IN THE MOUNTAINS – THE BEAUTY AND BRUTALITY, ISBN: 978-1-4092-7674-6

101. YUSUF'S ODYSSEY, ISBN: 978-1-291-33902-4

102. WILD AND FREE, ISBN: 978-1-4452-0747-6

103. HATCHED FREE, ISBN: 978-1-291-37668-5

104. THROUGH PRICKLY SHRUBS, ISBN: 978-1-4092-7

105. BLOOMIN' SLUMS, ISBN: 978-1-291-37662-3

106. SPEEDBALL, ISBN: 978-1-4092-0521-0

107. SPIRALLING ADVERSARIES, ISBN: 978-1-291-35449-2

108. EXULTATION, ISBN: 978-1-4092-7483-4

109. FREAKY LANDS, ISBN: 978-1-4092-7603-6

110. TREE SPIRIT, ISBN: 978-1-326-29231-7

Andreas Sofroniou

111. MAN AND HIS MULE, ISBN: 978-1-291-27090-7

112. LITTLE HUT BY THE SEA, ISBN: 978-1-4478-4066-4

113. SAME RIVER TWICE, ISBN: 978-1-4457-1576-6

114. CANE HILL EFFECT, ISBN: 978-1-4452-7636-6

115. WINDS OF CHANGE, ISBN: 978-1-4452-4036-7

116. TOWN CALLED MORPHOU, ISBN: 978-1-4092-7611-1

117. EXPERIENCE MY BEFRIENDED IDEAL, ISBN: 978-1-4092-7463-6

118. CHIRP AND CHAT (POEMS FOR ALL), ISBN: 978-1-291-75055-3

119. POETIC NATTERING, ISBN: 978-1-291-75603-6

120. FREE WILL AND EXTISTENTIALISM, ISBN: 978-0-244-60079-2

121. INSTINCTS AND MECHANISM OF BEHAVIOUR, ISBN: 978-0-244-60468-4

122. PROCESSES OF THINKING. CREATIVITY AND IDEOLOGIES, ISBN: 978- ISBN: 978- 0-244-91126-3

123. PHILOSOPHY AND SCIENCE OF ESCHATOLOGY, ISBN: 978-0-244-63224-3

124. SCIENCE FICTION THE WONDER OF HUMAN IMAGINATION, ISBN: 978-0-244-93409-5

125. HISTORY OF COMPUTER PROGRAMS, ISBN: ISBN: 978-0-244-64246-4